More Praise for

THE TYRANNY OF VIRTUE

"Robert Boyers writes in the great tradition of Saul Bellow, Irving Howe, and Susan Sontag: a powerfully persuasive, insightful, and provocative prose that mixes erudition and firsthand reportage, combativeness and sympathy, moral vehemence and humor. From his vantage point as long-time editor of the preeminent journal *Salmagundi*, Boyers has been in close contact with every seismic shift in literary, intellectual, artistic, and academic quarters in recent decades, and for those of us who may require guidance, here is our guide."

—Joyce Carol Oates

"Robert Boyers's voice is a bracing one: courageous, unsparing, and nuanced to a rare degree. In this book, he patiently and wittily speaks sanity to the towering forces of cultural craziness, and he actually respects everyone—well, nearly everyone—whom he subjects to his rigorous critique. For anyone wondering how a person should be, *The Tyranny of Virtue* is an excellent example."

—Mary Gaitskill

"This is a moment in which many robust voices claim attention for groups and causes that have been undervalued historically—a splendid moment for a culture that, at its best, places great value on reform that tends toward justice. In our universities, the debates it encourages have sometimes become vitriolic and judgmental. Robert Boyers has given us a reminder of the complexity of the issues at stake and the urgency of preventing a humane impulse from being overwhelmed by passions unworthy of it."

—Marilynne Robinson

"*The Tyranny of Virtue*: think of virtue as an ideal, and yet also as a tyranny, and all that does not belong to that realm must cower and disappear. We live in a time when true virtue seems to have disappeared, and everything that is not virtuous has taken to wearing virtue as a cloak. Of course I might have begun by saying that I know of almost no one but Robert Boyers who can succinctly penetrate and dispose of this masquerade of a period we are living in. So much that is wrong and dark he reveals in extraordinarily limpid prose, showing us that what is out there will not be made right and clear without the courage to name the human mess we have made. The life of the academy should remain sacred, and this book makes a splendid case for it, for the proposition that virtue is permanently hinged to the ideal of truth—that many-hued and illusive reality. The admirable and triumphant accomplishment of this work is that it adds to the ongoingness of our common enterprise. *The Tyranny of Virtue* is a wonderful book, and I shall always have it nearby."

—Jamaica Kincaid

"For decades Robert Boyers has been a bracing voice of sanity amid the ideological fashions of left and right. *The Tyranny of Virtue* is vintage Boyers—a brave and timely challenge to the suffocating moral orthodoxy that has come to envelop academic life and much of our broader public discourse as well. No one who cares about the future of independent thought can afford to ignore this book."

—Jackson Lears, Board of Governors
Distinguished Professor of History,
Rutgers University

"Boyers's assessment is all the more persuasive for the way it draws on his own long experience as a teacher, critic, and commentator on American culture."

—David Bromwich, Yale University

"Robert Boyers has written a probing meditation on his experiences within the left-liberal cultural bubble, including his own college, where he has been a formidable presence for decades. He trenchantly challenges assumptions, slogans, and nostrums of those excessively certain and proud of their 'wokeness.' I found *The Tyranny of Virtue* to be instructive and inspiring."

—Randall Kennedy, Michael Klein Professor
of Law, Harvard University

THE
TYRANNY
OF VIRTUE

IDENTITY, THE ACADEMY,
AND THE HUNT FOR
POLITICAL HERESIES

ROBERT BOYERS

SCRIBNER
New York   London   Toronto   Sydney   New Delhi

Scribner
An Imprint of Simon & Schuster, Inc.
1230 Avenue of the Americas
New York, NY 10020

First Scribner trade paperback edition November 2021

SCRIBNER and design are registered trademarks of The Gale Group, Inc.,
used under license by Simon & Schuster, Inc., the publisher of this work.

For information about special discounts for bulk purchases,
please contact Simon & Schuster Special Sales at 1-866-506-1949
or business@simonandschuster.com.

The Simon & Schuster Speakers Bureau can bring authors to your live event.
For more information or to book an event, contact the Simon & Schuster Speakers
Bureau at 1-866-248-3049 or visit our website at www.simonspeakers.com.

Interior design by Kyle Kabel

Manufactured in the United States of America

1   3   5   7   9   10   8   6   4   2

Library of Congress Cataloging-in-Publication Data has been applied for.

ISBN 978-1-9821-2718-3
ISBN 978-1-9821-2719-0 (pbk)
ISBN 978-1-9821-2720-6 (ebook)

Grateful acknowledgment is made to the following publications in which several
chapters of this volume first appeared—though in most cases the earlier periodical
versions have been substantially altered: "Privilege for Beginners" in the *American
Scholar*, "The Academy as Total Cultural Environment" in the *Chronicle of Higher
Education*, "Correctness & Denial" in *Raritan*, "Hostile & Unsafe" in the *Chronicle
of Higher Education*, and "Policing Disability" in the *American Interest*.

For Peg Boyers
and for our friends and colleagues at Skidmore College—
they know who they are—who labor,
against heavy odds, to keep alive the liberal tradition

CONTENTS

A PREFACE

Bitter struggles deform their participants in subtle, complicated ways. The idea that one should speak one's cultural allegiance first and the truth second (and that this is a sign of authenticity) is precisely such a deformation.

—Zadie Smith

A student at a graduation party tells you she thinks you're "woke," and you say thank you and you're not sure you know what that means. "It's no small thing," she continues, "for an old white guy like you." And so you think further about it the next day. Try to process the idea. Obvious that you can talk the talk. Invoke the system and the market, inequality and abuse, neoliberalism and privilege. That you don't offend. After three classes with you the student probably means mainly that. You don't offend. Willing to talk politics when teaching your courses. Not averse to assigning books sure to provoke unrest. Michel Houellebecq and Claudia Rankine. Susan Sontag and Slavoj Žižek. Zadie Smith and Philip Roth. And yet no prospect, you think, that you'll spontaneously utter something that will lead decent people to walk out or turn their backs. Decent people. The kinds who sign up for your classes, attend your lectures, read your articles, and occasionally send you email letters to express their encouragement or disappointment. Even your kids, who are given to noting your deficiencies, assure you that you've written nothing to embarrass them—not yet, though they are wary of your insistence on coming out with things uncomfortable or contrarian. Your habit of criticism. Your tendency to quarrel with people in your own left-liberal cohort. The pleasure you take in saying no to things many of your friends embrace. Maybe too reluctant to let people know you're with them. Pissed off about always needing to show your papers and confirm you're on board. Wanting to have it both ways. Wanting to be "woke" and yet disdainful of the rituals and empty posturing that signify your determination never to offend. In truth, if truth be told, not always on board even with what passes for the higher wisdom in your own herd of independent minds. Your friendly demeanor no longer sufficient to cover over the fact that you're unwilling to sit quietly, hands nicely folded, in the total cultural environment many of your friends and colleagues want to inhabit. Total, in that all are expected to speak with one voice about the right and the true. No misgivings permitted. An environment in which naysayers and dissidents are routinely asked to leave the room. Not always "asked," you say, wondering, not for the first time, how you can have avoided that fate yourself.

The resolve not to be swept off your feet, to avoid fanaticism and ideology, often ends in ambivalence. Nothing new in that. The standard caricature of liberals has it that they are unable to make judgments at all, that they are weak and irresolute. Boring.* That the best they can aim for is coexistence. Getting along with oppo-

* Susan Sontag: "Liberalism is boring, declares Carl Schmitt in *The Concept of the Political*, written in 1932 (the following year he joined the Nazi party)."

nents. Keeping open the channels of communication. Don't you ever feel sick and tired of pushing tolerance? A question put to you late one night by venerable provocateur Stanley Fish at a New Year's Eve party in Miami Beach. Fish notorious for promoting the caricature of liberals as people who want the mind to be empty of commitments, who are paralyzed by principles. You tell him you're amazed he still promotes this nonsense, that he's been peddling this caricature for so many years that he actually believes it. He says, amiably, that if you're willing to stand and fight, you should just stop calling yourself a liberal. Admit there are things you won't negotiate. You laugh. Tell him you're always willing to talk. And fight. In the university, you tell him, to refuse to talk is to give up the game. A liberal who's willing to fight is a contradiction in terms, he says.

In fact, you've been a partisan in the ongoing culture wars for about thirty years. Troubled by the turn in liberal culture toward what Fish calls "structures of exclusion." Trying to square your liberal principles with your sense that people who are with you on most things—on the obligation to move the world as it is closer to the world as it should be—are increasingly suspicious of dissent. Bizarre, of course, that of all places the liberal university should *Especially galling are the mandated sessions with lawyers and bureaucrats designed to generate an atmosphere of unanimity.* now be the one where strenuous efforts are most emphatically made to ensure consensus. Your own efforts in recent years having mainly to do with attempting to understand how people who are as adept as you are at arguing ideas and reading books can have managed to sign on to protocols that are often intolerant and illiberal. Always you

wonder that these people—many of them amiable and well-read—
no longer incline to think about the fact, noted by political theorist
Stephen Holmes and many others, that "public disagreement [as]
a creative force may have been the most novel and radical principle
of liberal politics." Little question, is there, that there is not much
appetite for serious debate when the opposition is unintimidated.
You see it on their faces when someone comes out with something
even mildly provocative. The rare, playful, contradictory utterance
like a bad smell the mildest among them prefer not to acknowledge,
while others, a bit more honest, are increasingly adept at wielding the
familiar arsenal of dismissive epithets, invoking the not yet exhausted
vocabulary of surefire conversation stoppers. Privilege, power, hostile
environment. The really fierce apparatchiks poised to promote and
finish the essential ideological cleansing.

———

Like others you've by now had it with the so-called free-speech
controversies, which have been talked to death—especially by partisans of the right, who pretend that the well-publicized eruptions
of violence at Yale and Middlebury and other such places confirm
their own reactionary prejudices and proclivities. But occasional
efforts to disinvite controversial lecturers or disrupt classes are but
a small token of more important problems, which include not only
the demands for "safe spaces" but the widespread insistence on
rituals designed to affirm that teachers are okay with the formulas
favored by the most vocal cadres on campus, not to mention the
prescriptions sent down by university officials and human resources
professionals. Especially galling are the mandated sessions with
lawyers and bureaucrats designed to generate an atmosphere of

unanimity, the sense that everyone, from the newly arrived freshman student to the department chair and provost, will be eager, when asked, to provide the correct answers to every question and thereby to avoid dispute, controversy, or legal challenge.

Of course now and then, in spite of the strenuous efforts to create a total culture, some incident will upend the order of things for a day or a month, and you think that maybe this time the dueling factions will actually attempt to engage in serious talk and renounce the slogans. Will they perhaps become disgusted with their inclination to call out others who've failed to "check their privilege" and instead think about privilege as something other than a lethal put-down? Will there be, at least temporarily, a halt to the protocols designed to shame or bully susceptible students or colleagues? Any chance, you wonder, that those given to condemning and harassing people who've said "the wrong thing" or dared to teach an offensive book or film will stop performing their vulnerability and abandon the studied censoriousness now so pervasive in precincts of the contemporary liberal university?*

————————

You remember that you're by no means alone in lamenting what makes the criticism of your own cohort so painful and difficult. In part, you suppose, the situation in the academy has something to do with larger problems in liberal culture. The political thinker Michael Walzer contends that "no one on the left has succeeded in telling a story that brings together the different values to which we are committed and connects them to some general picture of what

* In *Winning the Race* the linguist and cultural critic John McWhorter speaks of "the self-indulgent joy of being indignant" and of "therapeutic alienation."

the modern world is like and what our country should be like." You take that in and you think that you would like to tell the story Walzer wants. And yet the trouble is that the values you embrace are not always compatible with one another. That the instinct to be charitable and forgiving is contradicted by the instinct to be critical and to call things by their rightful names. That the respect you accord to opponents can seem irresponsible when those opponents are themselves intolerant and are bent on shutting up people like you.

More troubling still, many of those in your cohort refuse to acknowledge that contradiction is an elementary fact of our common life, and are in denial about all the things their own avowals fail to take into account. Hard not to feel disappointed when brilliant law students at Harvard mobilize to forbid the use of the word "violate," or when students and teachers at Brandeis deploy the term "microaggression" to attack an installation designed to expose racial stereotypes.

Concepts with some genuine merit—like "privilege," "appropriation," and even "microaggression"—have been very rapidly weaponized.

Are there in fact microaggressions? No doubt. Are some people uncomfortable when we use ordinary terms like "violate" and thereby trigger in them unwanted thoughts? To be sure. But it is—it must be—legitimate to ask what is lost and what is gained when we capitulate to demands that have as their objective the cleansing of the common language and the creation of a surveillance culture.

When a lawyer at your own New York State Summer Writers Institute, working on a memoir about her own personal tribulations, mounts a public campaign against the screening of a "disturbing"

1960s Italian comedy that may trigger, in a person with her background, traumatic memories, you are courteous and sympathetic, and yet find that what counts for her is the opportunity to invoke a principle and to put others—yourself very much included—on the defensive. When you tell her that the principle she invokes—it's never a good idea to screen films that portray desire, abuse, or subordination—is not a principle you share, and that other students in the program clearly have an entirely different view of such matters, she tells you that as a man you'll never understand the problem. You wonder what such encounters reveal about the culture and about your own resistance to the kinds of complaint articulated by a person who is deeply invested in her convictions. A friend tells you that you must learn to relax. Avoid unnecessary agitation. Let small things be small things and move on. And if they're not small things? They're always smaller than you make them out to be, he says. That lawyer is symptomatic of nothing.

The attempt to create a total cultural environment and to silence or intimidate opponents is part of a campaign that had once seemed promising, even to those—yourself included—alarmed at the irrationality and anti-intellectuality unleashed by many of the most vocal proponents of the new fundamentalism. But concepts with some genuine merit—like "privilege," "appropriation," and even "microaggression"—were very rapidly weaponized, and well-intentioned discussions of "identity," "inequality," and "disability" became the leading edge of new efforts to label and separate the saved and the damned, the "woke" and the benighted, the victim and the oppressor. Concepts useful in careful and nuanced discussions proved strikingly "amenable to over-extension," as the cultural historian Rochelle Gurstein put it, and ideas suitable for addressing "psychological distress" were forced into the service of efforts to "[redress] the subordination of one people by another," yielding not significant redress but a new wave of puritanism and a culture of suspicion.

It's tempting to fall back on the notion that cultural battles are predictable and recurrent and that those who wage them are always apt to lose sight of what is truly important. Your middle son, a CEO and social justice activist in St. Louis, reminds you that speech codes and academic protocols distract you from what you know to be the major issues out there in the real world, and you argue, not always successfully, that "privilege," "toleration," "identity," and "appropriation" are in fact real-world issues. Different, to be sure, from equality or sexual violence or racism, but important. Even good ideas, you say, when they are misused and misunderstood, can create a toxic environment. And the university is, in many ways, an increasingly toxic environment. Toxic in what sense? your son asks. You'll read my book, you tell him, and you'll hear my stories, and follow out the arc of my thinking, for what it's worth. And you'll see that, as always, I'm mainly trying to identify and wrestle with my own uncertainties, while demanding that others do no less. And if they're not as doubt-filled as you are? Well, they should be, shouldn't they? you reply. Does it ever occur to you, he asks, that you put too high a value on doubt and contradiction? Let me get back to you about that, you say.

THE
TYRANNY
OF VIRTUE

PRIVILEGE FOR BEGINNERS

It kicked in early, my confusion.

—Allan Gurganus

. . . awareness gone massively awry.

—Phoebe Maltz Bovy

In my freshman year at Queens College I had a strange awakening—strange in that the attendant, overmastering emotion was a combination of humiliation and pleasure. My English professor had called me to his desk and handed me the A+ paper I had written on Orwell's *Homage to Catalonia* and suggested that I make an appointment to see him. This was no ordinary suggestion at the City University of New York, where professors never scheduled regular office hours and only rarely invited students to private conferences.

Of course I was uneasy about the meeting, though I thought it likely that Professor Stone wished simply to congratulate me further, perhaps even to recommend that I join the staff of the college literary magazine or to enlist my assistance as a tutor for students who needed help with their writing. Delusions of grandeur. Modest grandeur.

Professor Stone's office had been carved out of a ramshackle warren of semi-enclosed rooms in the fourth-floor attic of the English department building, where I was greeted with a warm handshake and a "delighted you could come" and a "just take a seat and wait for a moment." Though the encounter took place almost sixty years ago, I remember everything about it, remember the few books randomly scattered on a small wooden table, the neatly combed silver hair on the professor's head, and the amiable ironic eyes. Most clearly I remember the surprising moment when another professor named Magalaner was called in and stood next to Professor Stone, both men smiling and looming ominously over me, the point of the meeting now further shrouded in mystery, just for a minute, until I was asked to describe—in a few sentences or more, don't hesitate—the paper I'd written on Orwell.

Which of course I did, as commanded, picking up steam after the first few sentences of diffident preamble, until Professor Stone asked me to just stop, that's quite enough, and then turned to his colleague with the words "See what I mean?" and Magalaner replied, "Totally." At which the two men now at last pulled over the two chairs and sat down, close enough that our knees almost touched, and seemed to look me over, as if taking my measure, both of them smiling, so that again I speculated that perhaps I was to be offered a prize or a summer job or who knew what else.

"I've a feeling," Professor Stone said, "that you may be the first person in your family to go to college."

"It's true," I replied.

"You write very well," he offered.

"Very well," said Magalaner.

"But you know," Stone went on, edging his chair just a bit closer to mine, "I didn't call you here to congratulate you, but to tell you something you need to hear, and of course I trust that you'll listen carefully—with Professor Magalaner here to back me up—when I tell you, very plainly, that though you are a bright and gifted young fellow, your speech, I mean the sounds you make when you speak, are such that no one will ever take you seriously—I repeat, no one will ever take you seriously—if you don't at once do something about this. Do you understand me?"

I've told this story on several occasions over the years, told it to my teenage sister—now a psychotherapist in New York City—on that very first night, explaining what I understood: namely, that a man I admired, who had reason to admire me, thought that when I opened my mouth I sounded like someone by no means admirable, and that in truth, to an educated person, I perhaps sounded like an idiot, like someone uncouth and pathetic, who could make even his own carefully composed sentences on Orwell sound like nothing anyone would bother to take in.

Easy, of course, to accept that no one close to me would have mentioned this before, given that—presumably—we all shared this grave disability and failed to think it a disability at all, noticing, perhaps, that a man like Professor Stone didn't sound like anyone in our family simply because, after all, he was an educated man and was not supposed to sound or think like us.

In any event, at our momentous encounter in that fourth-floor attic room, my teacher moved at once to extract from me "a promise" that I would enroll in "remedial" speech courses "for the remainder of your college career" and not "so much as consider giving them up, not even if you find them tedious." A proposal that left me feeling oddly consoled, if also somewhat ashamed. Consoled by the thought that there might be a cure for my coarse "Brooklynese," as my teacher referred to it, and that the prescription was after all indisputably necessary. Unsure in the moment about whether to thank my interlocutors or just to stand up and slink ignominiously away, the best I could muster, after agreeing to enroll right away in one of those speech courses, was an awkward "Is that all?"

A former student, hearing my story a few years ago at our dinner table, after telling her own tale of a recent humiliation, asked, "Who the fuck did that guy think he was?" and added that he was "lucky you didn't just kick his teeth out." Concerned, clearly, that even now, after so many years, my sense of self might still be at risk, the injury still alive within me. And yet, though in truth I've often and insistently played out the whole indelible encounter in my head, I had decided, within hours of my escape from that dark, low-ceilinged space, that it was a never-to-be-forgotten gift I had been offered. An insult as well, to be sure, but delivered not with an intention to hurt but to save and uplift. Easy to be offended about the class element inscribed in the transaction, the attempt to impress on someone so young the idea that he would want, no question about it, to become the sort of person whose class origins would henceforth be undetectable, Professor Stone thus my very own Professor Higgins, stepping in to do something about the grotesquely unlovely sounds emitted by the promising young Eliza, with that dreadful little mouth. But I had not been programmed to be offended, and was, in my innocent way, ambitious, eager, at any rate, to be taken seriously, and though I rapidly came to loathe the speech exercises to which I was soon subjected, I thought it my duty and my privilege to be subjected to them. Night after night, standing before the mirror in my parents' bathroom, I shaped the sounds I was taught to shape, and I imagined that one day Professor Stone would beam with satisfaction at the impeccably beautiful grace notes I would produce.

A long story, perhaps, unduly long, it may be, for the opening of an essay on "privilege." But then, the idea of privilege has moved a great many people in the culture to say things nonsensical and appalling, and I've thought to begin by noting what is often ignored or willfully obscured: that privilege is by no means easy to describe or understand. Say, if you like, that privilege is an advantage, earned or unearned, and you will be apt to ask several important questions. Earned according to whom? Unearned signifying shameful or immoral? The advantage to be renounced or held on to? To what end? Whose? Privilege the name of an endowment without which we would all be miraculously released from what exactly? Evidence, anywhere, that the consciousness-raising directed in recent years at privilege has issued in a substantial reduction in inequality or created a more generous public discourse? Say "privilege" and you will likely believe you have said something meaningful, leveled a resounding charge, when in fact you may not think about what is entailed in so loaded a term. What may once have been an elementary descriptor—"he has the privilege of studying the violin with a first-rate music instructor"—is at present promiscuously (and often punitively) deployed to imply a wide range of advantages or deficits against which no one can be adequately defended.

Is privilege at the root of the story I have told about my adolescent adventure? Consider that Professor Stone was himself the beneficiary of the privilege, so-called, that allowed him to deliver a potentially devastating message to a boy he barely knew, and with little fear of contradiction. The protocols lately associated with what literary critic Phoebe Maltz Bovy calls the "privilege turn" in contemporary culture would demand that the professor acknowledge his privilege and proceed with perhaps greater sensitivity to the feelings of his student. In 1959, to be sure, had he been challenged, the professor would simply have noted that the action he took was a reflection of his concern for his student, and he would not have felt that there was any special privilege involved in the exercise of his authority. The fact that our positions were unequal would have seemed to him not only natural but also in no way problematic, in that this was in the very nature of the teacher-student relationship, and moreover reflected only a temporary arrangement, requiring of me no permanent resignation to my fate as a subordinate, consigned for all time to yield to the whims of a master.

In short, whatever the privilege entailed in the exercise of power enjoyed by my teacher, the very notion of privilege in his case would have seemed to him—quite as it seems to me now—of little or no importance. Of course, if I were so inclined, I might now level the charge at my teacher, retroactively, as it were. After all, inequality is today often regarded as unjust or intolerable, even criminal, in spite of the fact that in most ordinary life situations we have no particular reason to feel aggrieved. I recall noting to myself, in a brief period when I saw a psychotherapist, the profound inequality built into our situation. After all, I thought, I know nothing at all about the emotions of my palely imperturbable therapist, whereas he is forever asking me personal questions and drawing astounding conclusions about my so-called motives. Our ritual meetings were designed to make me feel that our relations were anything but reciprocal, and of course my analyst had the privilege of treating everything I said as suspect, or symptomatic, whereas I was required to treat the few things he said as mature and reliable. Again, the inequality was a constitutive feature of the situation, and if his was the position of the master, mine that of the subordinate, there was nothing for me to do but nurture my resentment or accept that I too enjoyed the very different privilege of placing myself in the hands of someone who might help me.

Privilege, then, like inequality, is not usually a simple matter. Not in the past, not at present, not even in the domain of male privilege, with all that particular species of entitlement entails. I suppose it fair to say that I know as much, and as little, about my own exercise of male privilege as most men who have enjoyed its benefits without sufficiently acknowledging them. But I suppose as well what it is also fair to say: namely, that the exercise of privilege among men is no unitary thing. My own working-class father had the privilege, after all, of working, through the best years of his adult life, in a Brooklyn dry-goods store for six days each week, from 8 a.m. to 9 p.m., fifty weeks each year. Would he have agreed, if alerted to the fact, that he was also the beneficiary of male privilege? I like to think that I could have persuaded him to accept that this was so, much though the two of us would then have gone on to reflect that his advantage, in that respect as in many others, was somewhat limited.

It is by no means a simple matter to speak of privilege in the domain of race relations. The black linguist John McWhorter notes that at present "the privileged status" enjoyed by white people—an idea rooted in fact and, to a great many of us, entirely obvious—has become a formula resistant to meaningful conversation, which fuels insupportable assumptions and resentments. "Your existential State of Living While White," McWhorter writes, "constitutes [for many in the academy] a form of racism in itself. Your understanding will serve as a tool . . . for something. But be careful about asking just what that something is, because that will mean you 'just don't get it.'" McWhorter deplores, among other things, the fact that the standard "White Privilege paradigm [is] more about feelings than action," and that proponents of the paradigm are unduly attached to "the idea that black people cannot solve their problems short of white people developing an exquisite sensitivity to how privileged they are." The public attention devoted to privilege seems to McWhorter to "shunt energy from genuine activism into—I'm sorry—a kind of performance art."

A few years ago I found myself embroiled in an argument at a symposium, where "white privilege" had been referred to by one speaker as a self-evident and unitary phenomenon. Was it really necessary, I asked, to point out that there is privilege and privilege, whiteness and whiteness? If my white colleague felt that she had a great deal to apologize for, and thought a public symposium a suitable occasion for a display of soul-searching, that was well and good, so long as she did not also suggest that we must all follow her lead and in fact feel about our own so-called privilege exactly what she felt. Was it reasonable to suppose that whiteness confers, on all who claim it, comparable experiences and privileges? Was my own background as a working-class Jewish boy, growing up in a predominantly black community, remotely similar to the background or disposition of a white colleague who had never known privation, or in fact had no contact at all with other black children? Did it matter, thinking of ourselves simply as possessors of white privilege, that one of us had written extensively on race issues while the other had devoted herself to scholarly researches on metaphysical poetry? Was it not the case, I asked, that what the poet Claudia Rankine calls "the boundaries" of our "imaginative sympathy" had been "drawn" in drastically different ways? How could whiteness, or blackness, signify to us the same things? To consider either of us *primarily* as white people, deliberately consigning to irrelevance everything that made us different from one another—and different from the kinds of white people who regard their whiteness as an endowment to be proud of—was to deny what was clearly most important about each of us. Rankine rightly challenges those who "argue that the imagination is or can be somehow free of race," and mocks white writers "who make a prize of transcendence," supposing that the imagination can be "ahistorical" or "postracial." But to insist that elementary distinctions be made, as between one experience of race and another, would seem indispensable to a serious discussion of privilege.*

Though whiteness was not an active or obvious factor in my encounter with Professor Stone, it is possible that, had I been a black student in his class, he might have resisted the impulse to call me in and inform me, in effect, that my speech seemed to him low or disreputable. In this sense, the mere fact of my whiteness, however unacknowledged by Professor Stone, would have conferred on me the inestimable advantage of having been chosen for the insult he directed at me. A peculiar advantage, to be sure. When I told my story to a half dozen student assistants recently, the two black students at our dinner table showered me with sympathy and asserted that they would have found the professor's admonition offensive and perhaps "done something about it." Though I attempted then to explain my own sense of the privilege afforded me, my students were by no means persuaded, and the white students

---

* The novelist Chimamanda Ngozi Adichie usefully ignited debate when she suggested, in a 2017 interview, that elementary distinctions are essential. Speaking of identity categories, and of privilege itself as a factor in definitions of trans identity, Adichie argued as follows: "If you've lived in the world as a man with the privileges that the world accords to men and then sort of change genders, it's difficult for me to accept that then we can equate your experience with the experience of woman who has lived from the beginning as a woman and who has not been accorded those privileges that men are." Though leading feminist writers have challenged Adichie's emphasis upon different experiences of privilege, her willingness to invoke experience is a refreshing rejoinder to those who suppose that distinctions rooted in "mere experience" are irrelevant.

at our table were sure only that things are different now than they were back then and that "respect" would now happily ensure that no professor would dare to do what my teacher had done.

A good many of my students, white and black, are in thrall to the idea that they are required to portray themselves as beautiful souls. Even those with little feeling for polemic or posturing are ever at the ready to declare—like their academic instructors—their good conscience and their attachment to the indisputably correct virtues. Thus they find in the idea of privilege an ideal vehicle. It seems at least to provide, to anyone who climbs on board, an opportunity to arrive at a sort of moral high ground that costs nothing. The students at my table were at one in feeling superior to my old teacher. He had, they felt, been oblivious to his privilege, and they were secure in their conviction that they would never be as oblivious as that. Their comfort lay in their unambivalent commitment to a species of one-upmanship. Theirs was the empty affirmation of an ideal they had no need to articulate with any precision, but which amounted to the certainty that, above all things, we are required to be and to remain perfectly guiltless. Nor did they recognize—not so that I could tell—that their immurement in good conscience was itself a privilege that could be secured only by finding others guilty, in one degree or another, of privilege.

Privilege had been invoked as a noise word intended to distract all of us from the substance of our discussion.

At a panel discussion on political fiction convened at the New York State Summer Writers Institute two years ago, a graduate student said that she associated the words "political fiction" mainly with male writers. By way of response, I suggested that much of the best political fiction was in fact written by women, and went on to name Doris Lessing, Nadine Gordimer, Ingeborg Bachmann, Pat Barker, Anita Desai, Joyce Carol Oates, and others about whom I myself had written in books and essays. At that, another graduate student raised her hand and, quivering with indignation, asked me whether I was aware of the privilege I had exercised in addressing the question. "Privilege" in what sense exactly? I asked. Your authority, she said, your presumption, the sense of entitlement that permits you to feel that you can pronounce on any question put to you. Not any question, I said. Only a question about which I actually have something potentially useful to say. But then of course, I added, I want, like you, to be alert to my own power, when I have any, and to be able to acknowledge that each of us, in a civilized setting like this one, is the beneficiary of several different kinds of privilege. Though no further fireworks then erupted, it was clear to pretty much everyone present on that occasion that privilege had been invoked as a noise word intended to distract all of us from the substance of our discussion and from the somehow unpleasant spectacle of a male writer intoning the names of great women writers, as if this were, in itself, a flagrant violation of a protocol. More, the invoking of "privilege" was oddly intended to punish the speaker of the offending words—my words—by making him into a representative of something he could not possibly defend himself against.

Privilege, then, is increasingly hauled in as a weapon, though wielded, in the main, by persons attached still to the conviction that, whatever their own bristling incivility and the punishing quietus they clearly intend to deliver, they remain in full possession of their virtue. Can those who come on, through all kinds of weather, as investigating magistrates with a brief to enforce really hope to regard themselves as generous and tolerant persons? The obsession with privilege has made the examining magistrate bit enticing to large numbers of those for whom being in the right is an article of faith.

In a recent interview, Zadie Smith speaks of her friendship with the writer Darryl Pinckney, describing him as "a model of . . . active ambivalence. He is as well read on African-American issues as anyone could imagine being," she goes on, and he "is absolutely aware that there is such a thing as having been subjected to the experience of blackness, which causes all kinds of consequences." Even so, Smith concludes, "at the same time, he claims the freedom of just being Darryl, in all his extreme particularity. I haven't met many people like that."

No need to observe—though I will—that the words "he claims the freedom of just being Darryl" denote the exercise of a privilege to which others would likewise hope to stake a claim, or that Smith is right to note that not many are now equipped to be "like that." There is privilege, of course, in the refusal to accede to someone else's view of you, the refusal to emit the affirming noises that declare unequivocally your willingness to be what others take you to be and insist that you remain. Not at all surprising that Smith has often described what she calls the "cartoon thinness" of many of the identity images we employ to certify who we are, or that a character in her recent novel *Swing Time* calls upon his friend to reevaluate her sense of reality with the words "You think far too much about race—did anyone ever tell you this?" Pinckney, of course—in spite of the great opening line of his novel *High Cotton* ("No one sat me down and told me I was a Negro")—has devoted virtually all of his writing to the study of race, and yet he has refused to think of himself principally as a race man. Though he is "absolutely aware," as Smith says, that race has marked him, his brave determination has been to affirm his "extreme particularity."

Again, no one will dispute the fact that in recent years, privilege has had largely to do with race. Neither will many dispute the fact that black writers who have challenged the standard racialist orthodoxies about color have often come in for withering criticism from other black intellectuals. When Ralph Ellison complained that black writers "fear to leave the uneasy sanctuary of race," he generated a firestorm of hostility. Even James Baldwin came in for considerable criticism, much of it having to do with his efforts to have it both ways; that is, to insist on his estrangement from the "white centuries" of Western culture while refusing to pretend that those centuries did not shape and define him. "I know, in any case," Baldwin famously wrote, "that the most crucial time in my own development came when I was forced to recognize that I was a kind of bastard of the West; when I followed the line of my past I did not find myself in Europe but in Africa . . . I brought to Shakespeare, Bach, Rembrandt . . . a special attitude. These were not really my creations, they did not contain my history. . . . At the same time I had no other heritage which I could possibly hope to use—I had certainly been unfitted for the jungle or the tribe. I would have to appropriate these white centuries, I would have to make them mine . . ."

Clearly Baldwin wears his ambivalences and refusals with the cunning of a man who is ever in search of what will suit him. He accords to himself, as he should, the privilege of fashioning what he calls "a special attitude," a "special place." Baldwin knew that he could not be the man he wished to be, or write the books he had to write, unless he found a personal way to declare "appropriate" affinities. He could not operate from a doctrinaire idea of ethnic solidarity, and thus was bound to provoke disappointment in quarters where solidarity was regarded as an indispensable virtue.

It's tempting to say of Baldwin that he was, after all, a great writer and that he was therefore singular in ways we ought not to claim for ourselves. But the drama he enacted, rooted in his "extreme particularity," is not so very alien to the condition most of us aspire to, however limited our courage and our gifts. Rankine notes that "we wish"—all of us—"to . . . unsettle the assumption that it is easy or simple to write what one 'is.'" But then, as she says, when we "keep familiar things familiar" we inevitably miss what is most important about ourselves. Baldwin's "special attitude" required that he repudiate familiar assumptions about what did and did not define him, and he accorded to himself the privilege of appropriating what he needed.

Of course Baldwin thought of the special place he was required to make for himself in terms peculiar to him and his situation. And why not? And yet, when I read the words "these were not really my creations," I find it impossible not to think that they apply as well to me, growing up in a working-class Brooklyn apartment without books or other cultural artifacts. Just so do I note that the words—Baldwin's words—"I might search in them in vain forever for any reflection of myself" are somewhat misleading, in that of course, like myself, he would early discover reflections of himself even in works far removed from his own family setting.

But what burns through every page of Baldwin's writing is the truth of his own intense subjectivity and his contempt for provincial slogans and categories, "provincial" a word notably absent from discussions of privilege, which rely on an impoverished idea of identity and, by extension, of what rightly belongs to each of us. The charge of privilege, as leveled even in ostensibly sophisticated critiques, carries with it the presumption that persons are readily intelligible, their natures and motives determined by accidents of color or class. When I read sentences that begin with the words "white persons think" or "whites can only know," I feel at once the fatal absence of any intimation of radical uncertainty. The agitation we want to feel in confronting the other—or in confronting what is opaque or impenetrable in ourselves—is denied, banished by the impulse to define and diminish by resorting to accusations of privilege, as if thereby the work of understanding might somehow be accomplished.

Does privilege in fact exist? Of course it does. Only a fool would deny that advantage is real and that some persons have what others lack. Though advantage is unevenly distributed in any population, or within any racial or ethnic group, it is legitimate to assert that whiteness has long been an advantage, however little some white people believe that their own whiteness has given them what others lack. Just so, we have reason to assert that there are other kinds of privilege that often determine, unfairly, the way people live, and suffer or thrive. But then, these are commonplaces, and if not everyone is as yet prepared to acknowledge them, that is hardly a good reason to employ "privilege" in the way it has lately been used. The culture of grievance that has taken shape in recent years has led to what Bovy calls "the fetishization of powerlessness" and the not always "polite bigotry" that makes it acceptable to target groups or persons not because of what they have done but because of what they are.

The most promising feature of the sudden infatuation with privilege was the focus not on the kinds of privilege everyone can see for themselves—expensive private schools, ten-bedroom vacation homes, inordinate tax breaks or deductions available only to the wealthy—but on advantages unacknowledged and pernicious. For a while it seemed a good idea to dwell on the hypocrisies that allowed us to proceed as if class inequities were not major factors in the system that supported our habits and assumptions. We were moved to learn things we wanted somehow not to learn: that housing laws designed to help returning GIs discriminated against black veterans; that college admissions boards, even where inclined to diversify their student bodies, continued to rely on protocols that would ensure acceptance mainly for the wealthy or the otherwise privileged; that apparently trivial slights or insults might conceivably affect people in disastrous ways, while allowing those responsible for the insults to proceed as if nothing consequential had transpired. Rankine argues that "whiteness has veiled from them their own power to wound," and though what she calls the "recourse to innocence: I did not mean to do any harm" has rightly been called out within the framework of "privilege," it is surely legitimate to ask where this initially promising thrust has taken us.

There is comedy in the rush of the well-heeled and enlightened to affirm their virtue by signaling their guilt.

For one thing, it has taken us to the domain of cliché and pure assertion. Nothing is easier than to wield the charge of privilege and thereby to win instant approval, nothing easier than to beat oneself up now and then for enjoying privilege while pretending to solidarity with the disadvantaged. There is comedy in the rush of the well-heeled and enlightened to affirm their virtue by signaling their guilt and their difference from those who have not yet mastered the rituals of self-disparagement and privilege-bashing required of them. And there is temptation, surely, in the prospect of constructing a privilege-free profile: in my case, for example, by citing my own less-than-exalted childhood in Bedford-Stuyvesant, my struggles in three years of remedial speech courses, not to mention the fact that I could never have succeeded in life by virtue of good looks or a soothing, impressively masculine baritone voice. Thus, competitively speaking, in the precinct shaped by the privilege obsession, here I stand, nearly virtuous, though white, to be sure, and though not completely powerless, near enough to having been so to qualify for a modicum of sympathy.

The absurdity inherent in all of this should not obscure the damage it has wrought: damage in sowing confusion even about the obvious—about the difference between what is important and less important, between doing what is injurious and being deficient in doing what is positively good, between sponsoring injustice and simply living more or less modestly in an imperfect world. To be unable to make these kinds of elementary distinctions is to be radically impaired, and there seems to me no question that the tendency to invoke privilege has exacerbated that impairment. There was, at the heart of the privilege critique, an enlightenment project. But the partisans committed to promoting and extending that critique are mainly interested in drawing hard lines separating the guilty from the saved, the serenely oblivious from the righteous, fiercely aggrieved, and censorious.

It is hard not to see in all of this the operation of garden-variety envy, though the online diatribes denouncing the guilty are necessarily loath to mention that sentiment, even where it is impossible to miss. At my own college, younger faculty have complained, on the record, about the "privilege" exhibited by faculty members who speak at length and "with confidence" about controversial matters. The charge carries with it the wish, sometimes the suggestion, that those "other" faculty members find a way to be ashamed of this privilege, which so many of their colleagues do not enjoy. Thus the very air of forthrightness and self-assurance can be made to seem as offensive and illegitimate as the Bentley parked ostentatiously in a well-tended driveway. Again, the rage to call out privilege is often an expression of a simple desire to have what others have, or to cast aspersions on those who have it. Not at all surprising that the most brilliant and accomplished of my colleagues should lately have inspired criticism that cites her "relentless articulacy" and her "always having something to say."

Also hard not to see that one consequence of the obsession with privilege is the growing divide within communities otherwise united by shared principles. The emphasis on so-called microaggressions, that is, on what Rankine calls "slippages," including the failure to acknowledge privilege, has created a climate in which many people have withdrawn from active participation in public or political life. Many faculty at my college have intimated, or declared, that they will no longer become involved in controversial debates or speak on the floor at faculty meetings. Why get involved in efforts to raise consciousness among students by enlisting in voter registration campaigns when some students will likely accuse you of exploiting your power and your privilege? Why join your local Democratic Party and work to field a slate of electable candidates in a swing district—a district that some of the time votes Republican—when you are apt to be pilloried for the privilege entailed in championing moderation and electability? After all, only someone privileged enough (and clueless enough) to embrace a gradualist approach to politics would counsel incrementalism. Better to stay out of politics entirely, with the privilege put-down always apt to erupt and make you feel guilty more or less as charged.

For that matter, why attempt to find common ground in situations where envy for your good fortune and resentment of your advantages are sure to make everything you do an expression of your "privilege"? For all the intensity unleashed by proponents of the privilege critique, they would seem to have little interest in real-world politics, that is, in coalition building and respect for difference. The tendency to think of potential allies as inevitably tainted by the habits and perspectives of their racial, ethnic, or gender cohort is unlikely to issue in an effectual politics. The privilege craze is part of a new fundamentalism built on a willful refusal to accept that the most obvious features of our so-called identity are the least reliable indicators of what may reasonably be expected of us.

None of this is to suggest that identity, as usually conceived, counts for nothing at all. "I am born," writes the philosopher Alasdair MacIntyre, "with a past; and to try to cut myself off from that past . . . is to deform my present relationships." At the same time, he goes on, "rebellion against my identity is always one possible mode of expressing it." We are always, as it were, moving forward from the condition and the tradition we inherit. A culture is in good order only when its people are engaged in conducting a continuous argument about the assorted goods they hope to pursue. The fundamentalism driving privilege as an *idée fixe* is predicated on the assumption of deficits inherent in groups and persons who are condemned to reflect those deficits and to apologize, however inadequately, for embodying them. That assumption is not only ungenerous. It is also, as a matter of simple fact, a lie, given that rebellion against aspects of identity is after all a quotidian feature of ordinary cultural evolution. The envy and resentment that would deny to Pinckney his "particularity" or to Baldwin his wayward "appropriation" or to W. E. B. Du Bois his will to "summon Aristotle and Aurelius and what soul I will" are no less vicious than promiscuous assertions of privilege deployed to deny the complex particularity of other persons. Proponents of the privilege argument have adopted a sanctimonious rhetoric to create an "us" and a "them" that answer not at all to the reality of our common life.

THE ACADEMY AS TOTAL
CULTURAL ENVIRONMENT

A university is among the precious things that can be destroyed.

—Elaine Scarry

*What to me is truly frightful is not the quality of what everyone
agrees on, but the very fact of universal agreement.*

—Alexander Nehamas

Three years ago, at the college I've been teaching at for a half century, a senior professor, the chair of the most powerful committee in the college, called for a special emergency meeting of the faculty (a so-called committee of the whole). He wanted to discuss a rumor he had heard about a secret letter apparently sent to the president by a dozen of his colleagues. The letter—so he had been informed—recommended that the president reconsider his plan to appoint a chief diversity officer, arguing that colleges should not endeavor to speak with one voice—not even on diversity issues—and that the decision to recruit a CDO had not been adequately discussed with the faculty.

In an email to the college faculty, the professor characterized the letter—which he insisted he had not read—as "divisive, exclusive, demoralizing, and disrespectful," and went on to declare "our community" an "inclusive" one in which "we are known for agreeing to disagree." Of course the professor did not—could not—engage at all with anything actually included in the letter, could not entertain the thought that at most institutions "diversity" does not refer to diversity of opinion, and that diversity officers are often appointed chiefly to ensure that a party line be promulgated and enforced. Neither could the professor respond to the proposition—also included in the letter he had not read—that college programs designed to foster an intense awareness of racial categories, whatever their virtues, may often generate unwanted results. Though he speculated that perhaps those who had signed the letter "were not really interested in race relations," he could not acknowledge that the signatories included prominent liberal intellectuals, some of whom had written extensively on race matters and successfully recruited black and minority faculty to teach at the college.

At the special meeting attended that afternoon by approximately two hundred faculty, in a packed college auditorium, the signatories to the offending letter were charged by assorted speakers with attempting to "obstruct" the efforts of the college to recruit minority faculty and students. Some faculty took the meeting as an occasion to speak—with restrained eloquence—of their own experience of discrimination, while others expressed incredulity at the "arrogance" of colleagues who had taken it upon themselves to address to the president questions about the effectiveness of existing programs in fostering the kind of community to which we presumably aspired. After all, as one particularly angry faculty member insisted, what could conceivably be said to defend any criticism directed at initiatives that had been officially approved by the relevant college committee?

The fact that the faculty members who leveled these charges had not read the letter in question in no way gave pause to those among them who raised their voices to express their outrage and yet also to affirm their allegiance to the idea of inclusiveness.

In spite of the charged atmosphere and sometimes incendiary rhetoric unleashed at the meeting, a few of the signatories to the letter identified themselves as such and responded to questions and attacks, wondering at the willingness of people to level wildly improbable and insupportable accusations while declaring themselves entirely igno-rant of what had actually been written in the letter to the president. For a while discussion focused on whether or not a letter intended to be "private" should remain so, even if some or all of the signatories insisted that the right to privacy was an important principle, not to be lightly dismissed. Late in the meeting, one youthfully ardent assistant professor stood up to propose, in a clear, confident voice, that "the authors of the letter apologize to everyone in this room even if they had no bad intentions and the letter they wrote doesn't specifically say what it is rumored to say." No misgiving there, no uneasiness about what she herself characterized as "the murkiness of the facts in the case," simply the certainty that those officially in the right, as they supposed, must affirm their enlistment in the truth and insist that those who had offended others know themselves to be outside the circle of the saved.

Though most people in our faculty did not weigh in on either side of this dispute, the meeting I've outlined reveals a great deal about the shape of things in American academic life. The professors who raged and postured were content to whip themselves into a fury of indignation about a letter they had not read. Those who had dared to raise questions about the college's commitment to a diversity that did not adequately allow for "a diversity of ideas," and noted that the college's program in intergroup relations had not been adequately subjected to the kind of debate routinely accorded to other college programs, were seen as challenging an indisputably correct consensus.

Which consensus? The one that takes it to be an unconscionable violation of propriety to raise serious questions about anything that has even remotely to do with race or identity when the relevant issues have been officially agreed on by a duly constituted, administratively sanctioned program or committee. The signatories to the letter might well have welcomed the appointment of a chief diversity officer had they believed that a new CDO would have a mandate to foster true intellectual diversity on campus and to oppose the subordination—of students and faculty alike—to an entrenched dogma. But the campus climate was such as to make that an unlikely prospect.*

The words uttered by the senior professor who had unleashed the fury—"we are known for agreeing to disagree"—were of course intended to disguise the obvious fact that disagreement is the last thing that many influential faculty members are today prepared to honor or tolerate. So deep and pervasive is the regime of intolerance to which large numbers of ostensibly liberal professors subscribe that they cannot acknowledge what has taken hold of them. The good professor who characterized the offending letter and, by extension, its signatories as "divisive" and "demoralizing" was unwittingly giving voice to a sentiment widely shared in the American academic community. To challenge officially accredited views, particularly when those views have anything to do with sensitive issues, is now regarded as out of bounds, illegitimate, an expression of arrogance or entitlement, and thereby hostile.

---

* In fact, the CDO whose appointment was announced just as the "Committee of the Whole" was convened, turned out to be an eminently thoughtful and compassionate person, though his efforts to disinfect the noxious political air have been only occasionally successful. As Cass Sunstein notes, "like-minded people [largely] insulated" from those with disparate views are apt to be moved by "parochial influences" and to insist upon talking "only to one another."

The fact that the challenges to the accredited consensus most often come from persons who are themselves liberals or progressives and, moreover, known to be invested in battles for diversity and a wide range of other standard liberal causes, only makes their deviation more enraging to inflamed partisans, for whom inclusiveness requires that all of their colleagues unambiguously subscribe to the dominant orthodoxy. As the philosopher Judith Butler once wrote, "the more rigid the position, the greater the ghost [that is, the possibility of being haunted by what's excluded], and the more threatening it is in some way."

It is tempting to describe the battles convulsing American campuses with epithets like "the politics of hysteria." In the United States especially, self-described liberal academics continue to believe that they remain committed to difference and debate, even as they countenance a full-scale assault on diversity of outlook and opinion, enwombed as they are in the certainties enjoined on them by the posture they have adopted, which alone confers on them the sense that they are always in the right.

Confront contemporary left-liberal academics—I continue to regard myself as a member of that deeply troubled cohort—with a familiar passage from John Stuart Mill's *On Liberty* and they will be moved at once to proclaim that Mill espouses what virtually all of us have long taken for granted. OF COURSE we understand that the tyranny of the majority must be guarded against—even when it is *our* majority. OF COURSE we understand that "the peculiar evil of silencing"—or attempting to silence—"the expression of an opinion is, that it is robbing . . . posterity as well as the existing generation; those who dissent from the opinion, still more than those who hold it. If the opinion is right, they are deprived of the opportunity of exchanging error for truth: if wrong, they lose . . . the clearer perception and livelier impression of truth, produced by its collision with error." What can be more obvious than that? OF COURSE we understand that there is danger in abiding uncritically with the views of one's own party or sect or class. Who among us doesn't know that even ostensibly enlightened views, shared with other well-educated persons like ourselves, cannot entitle us to think of those views, or of those who hold them, as infallible?

And yet a good many liberal academics are not actually invested in the principles to which their avowals ostensibly commit them. Mill noted among his own contemporaries, more than 150 years ago, what is very much in evidence in our own culture, namely, that certain opinions have come to seem so important to society that their usefulness cannot be legitimately challenged. Thus a great many contemporary liberals subscribe to the belief—however loath they may be to acknowledge it—that certain ideas are heretical and that those who dare to articulate them must be, in one way or another, cast out. The burning desire to paint a scarlet letter on the breast of those who fail to observe the officially sanctioned view of things has taken possession of many ostensibly liberal persons in the academy, which has tended more and more in recent years to resemble what the cultural critic David Bromwich calls "a church, held together by the hunt for heresies."*

---

* Wesley Yang notes that at schools like UC Berkeley a "list of microaggressions [is] circulated to Professors" and that the list includes "America is a land of opportunity" and other such expressions regarded as "so pernicious" that university officials "no longer believe that they should be engaged with, debated, or debunked." As of 2017, Yang reports, "Two hundred thirty-one universities now have 'bias response teams' that investigate the speech of professors and students, often with the aid of campus police officers, for infractions that include microaggressive speech." What is unfortunate is not the fact that people are asked to be sensitive to bias but what Yang calls "the manner in which activists are seeking to win a debate—not through scholarship, persuasion, and debate . . . [but] through the subornation of administrative and disciplinary power to delegitimize, stigmatize, disqualify, surveil, forbid, shame, and punish holders of contrary views."

When Mill wrote of the threat to liberty of "thought and discussion," he was responding, at least in part, to Tocqueville's idea that in modern societies the greatest dangers to liberty were social rather than legal or political. Both men believed that the pressures to conform, and the pleasures associated with conformity, were such that these societies would not find it necessary to burn heretics at the stake. Mill explained:

And thus is kept up a state of things very satisfactory to some minds, because, without the unpleasant process of fining or imprisoning anybody, it maintains all prevailing opinions outwardly undisturbed, while it does not absolutely interdict the exercise of reason by dissentients afflicted with the malady of thought. . . . But the price paid for this sort of intellectual pacification, is the sacrifice of the entire moral courage of the human mind. A state of things in which a large portion of the most active and inquiring intellects find it advisable to keep the genuine principles and grounds of their convictions within their own breasts.

Sad to say, however, the expectations nowadays enforced with increasing and punishing severity in various contemporary institutions—most notably in the academy—are somewhat more alarming than the regime Mill described. While dissentient views are today not always absolutely interdicted, and we do not hear of persons who are imprisoned for espousing incorrect views, we do routinely observe that "active and inquiring intellects" are often cast out of the community of the righteous by their colleagues and, in cases that have received national attention, formally "investigated" by witch-hunting faculty committees and threatened with the loss of their jobs. One need only mention, once again, the widely debated incidents at Middlebury College or Northwestern University or the Evergreen State College, among many others,* to note that this is by no means a phenomenon limited to a handful of institutions. The fact that these eruptions have often drawn wildly inaccurate and misleading coverage in the right-wing media should not distract us from the serious implications of the kinds of intolerance promoted by ostensibly liberal faculty. The influential faculty member at my own college who called the special meeting to expose the dozen professorial wrongdoers hoped to stir the kind of outrage that would be an object lesson to the community and deter potentially divisive persons from provoking the ire of their colleagues in the future. Such show trial–like events are the leading edge of efforts to create what the critic Lionel Trilling once called "a total cultural environment" built on "firm presuppositions, received ideas, and approved attitudes."

What does "a total cultural environment" look like? In the university it looks like a place in which all constituencies have been mobilized for the same end, in which every activity is to be monitored to ensure that everyone is on board. Do courses in all departments reflect the

* The eruptions have been stirred by students, faculty, and administrators alarmed by so-called threats to the psychological safety of community members. At Evergreen State the threat was embodied by a professor of biology (subsequently forced to resign from the faculty) who criticized the university's "Day of Absence," on which all white students would be asked to leave the campus. At Northwestern a professor was subjected to a formal Title IX investigation by university authorities after an essay she wrote for the *Chronicle of Higher Education* was said by a number of students to create "a hostile environment" on campus. At Middlebury hundreds of students and faculty shut down a lecture by a controversial scholar and fomented violence to protest what they called "hate speech." Needless to say, these incidents—like comparable incidents at Yale and other schools—have been furiously debated.

commitment of the institution to raise awareness about all of the approved hot-button topics? If not, something must be done to address that. Are all incoming freshmen assigned a suitably pointed, heavily ideological summer reading text that tells them what they should be primarily concerned about as they enter? Check. Does the college calendar feature—several times each week, throughout the school year—carefully orchestrated consciousness-raising sessions led by human resources specialists trained to facilitate dialogues leading where everyone must agree they ought to lead? Check. Do faculty recognize that even casual slippages in classroom or extracurricular discourse are to be met with condemnation and repudiation? See to it. Is every member of the community primed to invoke the customary terms—"privilege," "power," "hostile," "unsafe"—no matter how incidental or spurious they seem in a given context? Essential. Though much of the regime instituted along these lines can seem—often does seem—kind and gentle in its pursuit of what many of us take to be a well-intentioned indoctrination, the impression that control and coercion are the name of the game is really hard to miss.

Of course there are those who will defend the emergent "total culture" by arguing that we know very well how devastating bias and other forms of abuse or violence can be, and thus that we have an obligation to mobilize to prevent them. And of course it is impossible to deny that such things continue to exist, and that efforts to raise awareness about them in an academic setting are indispensable. Even those of us who are worried about the future of liberal education, and about regimes of intolerance on the nation's campuses, have often acknowledged, with however many reservations, that speech codes can be a good and necessary thing. I've never met an academic—liberal or conservative—who believes that we should give a pass to racists who openly spread their poison in a classroom. When Donald Trump complains of the protocols and protections mandated to ensure that workplace and academic environments protect their citizens from flagrant abuse or intimidation, and declares these safeguards a laughable species of political correctness, we observe that he and his friends do not understand the relationship between freedom and responsibility, between open discussion and the civility that alone makes real discussion possible.

But things have gotten out of hand. A recent column by Nicholas Kristof of the *New York Times* argues that many liberals "want to be inclusive of people who don't look like us—so long as they think like us." On campuses across the country, according to Kristof, academics casually admit that "they would discriminate in hiring decisions" based on "the ideological views of a job applicant." For many academics, the desire to cleanse the campus of dissident voices has become something of a mission. A distinguished scholar at my own college writes in an open email letter to the faculty that when colleagues who are "different" (in his case nonwhite, non-straight, non-male) speak to us, we are required not merely to listen but to "validate their experiences." At a faculty reception a week or so later a colleague asks what I think of the open letter, and I tell him I admire the guy's willingness to share his thoughts but have been puzzling over the word "required" and the expression "validate their experiences." Does he mean thereby to suggest that if we have doubts or misgivings about what a colleague has said to us we should keep our mouths firmly shut? Exactly, replies my earnest, right-minded companion, who can't believe that I have any trouble with that.

In the last year or two, those wishing to restrain real talk or, God forbid, actual debate more and more deploy terms like "entitlement" and "subordination" to suggest that people who stir the waters inevitably create a "hostile environment" and intimidate their colleagues, some of whom—so it is said—are thereby made to feel powerless.

In this context, the term "entitlement" refers to people who have the confidence to speak with conviction and independence. The implication, unmistakable here, is that only those with power can speak, and that when they do so, they inevitably silence or strike fear into the hearts of every-one else, which includes the overwhelming majority of those who acquiesce in the established consensus. Not acknowledged in this scenario, though it ought to be obvious to anyone who actually values debate and difference, is that the "entitlement" belongs to all of those willing to speak out, and to take the heat, and to proceed without taking it for granted that what they say will be applauded. The puerile notion that only those who are powerful and secure will ever feel entitled to speak out is one of those unfortunate assumptions promoted by those who want to be protected from actually having to confront controversy or discomfort.

Deviations once regarded as signs of a robustly diverse intellectual climate come more and more to seem intolerable.

Though it must seem odd to those who spend little or no time in the academy to hear that academic intellectuals are notoriously susceptible to groupthink, there are several compelling ways to account for this. For one, as the psychologist Jonathan Haidt has pointed out in *The Righteous Mind*, academics are much like other people in "trying harder to *look* right than to *be* right" when they conduct an argument. Within the confines of a community that is apt to pride itself on its disciplined commitment to a consensually agreed-on set of "enlightened" views, deviations once regarded as signs of a robustly diverse intellectual climate come more and more to seem intolerable, given the strenuous efforts of the community to create a "total culture."

Though new ideas, new evidence, unfamiliar works may now and then briefly challenge the comfortably accredited views underwriting the official stance of academic institutions—think of the creative turmoil provoked by the writings of Thomas Kuhn, Jacques Derrida, Michel Foucault, and Elaine Showalter a generation ago—the "confirmation bias" described by the psychologist Peter Wason will typically ensure that new ideas, no matter how compelling, will be received only in ways that confirm the enlightened consensus. A wide range of psychological tests conducted by Wason and others cited by Haidt provide no evidence whatsoever that the professoriate is any more likely than a less educated cohort to think independently, that is, to process fresh ideas and to draw from them anything but the officially sanctioned conclusions.

Academics today are increasingly behaving like members of an interest group.

As Wason and other psychological researchers note, academics tend to have higher-than-average IQs and are predictably "able to generate more reasons" to account for what they believe. But high-IQ people like academics typically produce "*only [a greater] number of my-side arguments*" and "are no better than others at finding reasons on the other side." This is especially troubling—or ought to be especially troubling—in the culture of the university, where diversity of outlook and idea, and resistance to accredited formulas, is at least theoretically central to the institutional mission.

But academics today are increasingly behaving like members of an interest group whose opinions they hold and value primarily as tokens of membership in the high-status, politically virtuous elite to which they subscribe. It was once possible to suppose that this particular interest group—given its ostensible commitment to education—would want to promote genuine diversity of opinion, if only to weaken the "confirmation bias" we all share, "a built-in feature" of what Haidt calls our "argumentative mind." But the ideological intolerance in the liberal academy at present is such as to make the confirmation bias seem to most academics not a danger but an entirely desirable feature of our collective enterprise.

Of course the intolerance is disturbing in a whole variety of ways and represents for many of us a threat to institutions of higher learning and to the work we hope to do as educators. But it is well to remember that, like other intellectual formations, our present troubles have a history. In the early 1950s, in the book *Political Ideas in the Romantic Age*, Isaiah Berlin identified what he called "a common assumption" informing the work of Enlightenment thinkers: "that the answers to all of the great questions must of necessity agree with one another." This "doctrine," Berlin argued, "stems from older theological roots" and refuses to accept any suggestion that we must learn to live with irresolvable conflicts. The consequence? The English political philosopher John Gray calls it "a monistic philosophy that opened the way to new forms of tyranny."

The word "tyranny" may seem extravagant as a description of tendencies at work in the contemporary academy, and yet, when we speak of the attempt to create "a total culture," dedicated to promoting a perfect consensus, we may well feel that we are confronting a real and present danger. The danger, for example, that context and complexity will count for nothing when texts or speech acts become triggers for witch hunts, and when wit and irony are regarded as deplorable deviations from standard protocol. "Tyrants always want language and literature that is easily understood," Theodor Haecker observes. At my own college, when a senior colleague at a public meeting last fall uttered an expression ("in their native habitat") felt by some auditors to be offensive—though clearly not intended to be so, and unmistakably ironic, and followed by a clear apology when a complaint was voiced—there were calls for her to resign from the faculty, and though she is, and will remain, with us still, the incident prompted a volley of abusive and self-righteous email rhetoric, drove more than one faculty member to advise students away from courses taught by "that woman," and stirred a renewed emphasis on "reeducation" and "rehabilitation."

Astonishing, of course, that those very terms—"reeducation" and "rehabilitation"—do not scare the hell out of academics who use them and hear them. That they do not call to mind the not-so-distant history of authoritarian regimes in Europe or lead on to the thought that "diversity," for many of us in the academy, has now come to mean a plurality of sameness. More important: the words, apparently, do not suggest how vulnerable we are—all of us—to error, slippage, and hurt, and how the protocols, tribunals, and shamings currently favored by many in the academy have distracted us from our primary obligation, which is to foster an atmosphere of candor, good will, kindness, and basic decency without which we can be of no use to one another or to our students.

CORRECTNESS & DENIAL:
WILLING WHAT CANNOT BE WILLED

We denied it . . . therefore none of it had happened.

—Howard Jacobson

Ask anyone to say something about "the will" and you will confirm that it is by no means an unfamiliar subject. Even those who profess to have little interest in it must admit that the idea has been useful to them at one point or another. Useful how? Often in accounting for some improbable phenomenon. For the man who managed through untiring effort to win the love of a woman unlikely to find him plausible. For the mediocre student who studied and managed somehow to achieve on a final examination a grade beyond anything he or his instructor might have predicted. All of us have heard of such things and remarked on the exertions required to accomplish what seemed out of reach. And thus we have thought of the will as a faculty that is, in one degree or another, part of our standard human equipment, and wondered occasionally why a wide assortment of thinkers have regarded the will as an obscure or puzzling notion.

But I'm drawn here not to the reflections of thinkers like Freud or Nietzsche but to humble anecdotage, to a summertime side street in a small town—call it Saratoga Springs—to an incident, at once tiny and inconsequential, with a five-year-old boy—let's call him

Lowell Boyers—kicking a soccer ball against the slats of a raised wooden porch, his father seated near him on a ladderback chair, idly turning the pages of a newspaper. The potted geranium mildly rattles as the ball strikes an unsteady table leg, and in a moment of distraction the man lowers his paper and observes that the boy is no longer there on the porch, so that the man rises from his chair and sees, over the porch railing, that the boy has darted across the sidewalk and now stands frozen in the one-way street, staring helplessly at the ball, which has come to a stop under a car parked on the far side of the tree-lined street. What are you doing out in the middle of the road? the man shouts at the boy. I'm not out in the middle of the road, the boy answers, his eyes now turned to meet his father's eyes bearing down on him. But you're out in the road right now, and I want you to get up here this second, the father commands. But I'm not, I'm not in the road, the boy repeats, still frozen there, even as a car rolls up in his direction and halts, waiting for the boy to get out of the way. I'm not here, the boy says one last time, as the father at last steps down from the porch, runs out to the boy, and gently escorts his son onto the sidewalk.

As I say, a tiny thing, this episode, told and retold a hundred times in our family, occasionally with variations designed to make the father seem even more foolish and overbearing than he seemed to the son. The point of the tellings? It has principally to do with what we like to call a perfect moment, one in which an ordinary event reveals with indisputable clarity something essential.

In that perfect moment our son Lowell was in the grip of an imperious will that had decreed his utter subordination to a single objective. He was reduced, in effect, to denying what was most true and obvious, namely that he had done what was not to be done in exposing himself to danger. Caught in the act, he froze as if on a stage set, arms rigid at his sides, following a script that would seem to have demanded merely that he stare straight ahead and repeat his lines, as if by some miracle they might lift him out of his misery. On the walk back to the sidewalk and then up onto the porch, he seemed still caught in that spell of willing, his eyes anxious but dull, trained on what might have been some other unreal world, his steps mechanical, his temporary anguish at once pitiful and comical.

Of course it is not usually the case that persons who find themselves willing what cannot be willed can actually be made to confront, in the act, as it were, what they have been doing. Often we remain attached to the ways of willing because we enjoy the benefits conferred by our refusal to acknowledge the absurdity to which we have grown accustomed. In fact, we continue to will what cannot be willed and pretend that we are doing no such thing because everyone else around us is caught up in the same sort of self-deception, each of us determined not to notice how ridiculous we would seem even to ourselves if we acknowledged the obvious. Willing what cannot be willed is a habit we indulge because usually we have no one we trust to call out to us, admonish us, and lead us back to the sidewalk.

My understanding of the will was shaped in a decisive way by the work of the psychoanalyst Leslie H. Farber, who was, in the decade before his death in 1981, my closest friend. In his book *The Ways of the Will*, Les had written that "no cunning is required on the part of an adversary to bring such distress [as may be caused by willing what cannot be willed] into a frank and painful prominence." Though I was not my son's "adversary" in the incident I have recounted, my very presence occasioned his distress, brought it truly into a "frank and painful prominence." What to call my son's distress? Call it "anxiety," a term Farber recommends we use on such occasions. Say that anxiety is the effect of willing what cannot be willed when you are at least somewhat aware of the untenable condition you have created for yourself, when you sense that your relation to reality has been compromised. Reality itself is not only at risk at such moments but out of reach. Yeats captured this when he spoke of "the will trying to do the work of the imagination," imagination understood as the capacity to acknowledge what is actually possible for persons whose ambitions some of the time seem, even to them, unrealistic or delusional.

In my own case, there is my tendency to suppose that what I say—clearly, forcefully, unapologetically—will seem admirable and persuasive even when I can recall times past when I delivered my thoughts to audiences and found them less than receptive. In such instances, imagination might well assist me to acknowledge that my insistence, my way with facts and evidence, my determination to go against the grain, are likely not to impress everyone as I would wish. And thus I will feel a good deal of anxiety whenever I come before people, hectoring and insisting, as I am wont to do, my anxiety intensifying the more I deny that I have brought this frustration on myself and refuse to accept that there is no comfortable way out of these encounters.

Willfulness can assume a great many different forms. Consider, for a moment, the will to tell the truth, to be honest, a policy often recommended to good boys and girls everywhere. Most of us accept that in real life, as we like to say, honesty is not usually a good idea. We don't expect a reasonably sane president's diplomatic team, negotiating a nuclear deal with Iran, to be open and honest with those seated at the table across from them or with the American public. We don't want teachers to frankly share all of their impressions with students who seem to them not very bright. Nor do we think it a good idea for a wife who has lately been obsessed with an attractive young colleague to share with her husband the fact that much of the time her thoughts are focused on her dazzling and attentive prospect. Should the wife nonetheless insist that honesty is after all the best policy, we would readily conclude that her will to truth telling, her willfulness, had led to a corresponding paralysis of imagination—that is, an inability to so much as acknowledge the pain her honesty would conceivably cause her husband.

Willfulness is often a factor in other precincts, as in the creation or reception of works of art. We see this in works that seem to know, from the first, what they want to say, and say it. Works that know all too well what to underline and what to suppress, that proceed as if they were in thrall to a message that no aspect of the work must be allowed to contradict. And we see a related phenomenon in the case of readers who subscribe to a set of ideological imperatives and thus demand of a work that it be unambiguous, that it model a species of virtue that no reader will be able to miss. Such ideological readers will demand positive characters with whom a reader can happily identify, and demand that characters who are not properly virtuous or "enlightened" will have their negative status highlighted, their reliance on privilege or power or class unambiguously cited so that it will seem unforgivable. For such readers, works of art exist to confirm what the "enlightened" reader already knows, and works that celebrate their own will to unimpeachable virtue will seem the best of all possible works. Not for such readers the exercise of imagination whose primary objective is precisely to lure the heart away from safety.

Needless to say, artists and writers are at least as susceptible as anyone else to varieties of denial. Who among us has failed to note, now and then, a curious reversal of course in a novel or film, in which we detect what is perhaps a recoil from some implication the writer would rather not admit to or explore? The old-fashioned term used to describe this sort of thing is "self-censorship," which entails a suppression of inconvenient thoughts inspired by a will to win the good opinion of a reader. In such cases, we feel that the writer is pandering, currying favor, that the work itself has become subordinate to the project of avoiding anything potentially offensive. We dislike works of art that are made with too good an opinion of themselves and with an eye to winning the ideological approval of a particular audience. Of course we admire an artist's or writer's apparent command of every aspect of a work. But we also delight in the sense that the artist wishes to live dangerously, to set in motion elements that threaten to escape her control. We value the ongoing sense that the artist is willing to be surprised by elements that she cannot have anticipated or plotted, that she is willing to risk a swerve into the rank or unthinkable.

In his book entitled *Antoine's Alphabet*, Jed Perl writes the following: "The artist can never fully control his creation. The work of art eludes the creator's grasp, takes on (one hopes!) a life of its own. If the work of art is going to live, it must eventually turn its back on the artist, it must go its own way." And yet, to how many works can we say that Perl's description applies? Those of us who are not great artists know how hard it can be to allow something we have made to turn its back on us and go its own way. We know this, in a sense, at least, in our relations with our own children, in our will to shape them in accord with the benevolent plans we devise for their future. I knew, for each of my three sons, when it was time to let go, when I had to acknowledge that it was incumbent upon them to turn their backs on me if they were to go forward in a direction that was in effect assigned to them by the laws of their own individual nature. The drawing back thus required of me as a father had nothing to do with a withdrawal of interest or support, but with a determination not to will what clearly could not be willed. For I had no significant prospect of definitively and beneficially shaping my sons to my own exacting and coercive specifications. I have always known, I think, what damage parents can do when they think to deny to their children the legitimate exercise of their freedom. "They fuck you up, your mum and dad," as Philip Larkin memorably put it. "It's not heights I'm afraid of—it's parents," Mel Brooks says in the film *High Anxiety*. Remembering such observations, delirious and appalling, it's hard not to think of my fatherly self as an onlooker at a spectacle

Will declares that it is possible to admire what we do not admire and to love what we cannot love.

that must inevitably unfold according to its own laws, some of the time irresponsibly. And I remember, as well, Farber's observation that the many objects of my concern will not often comply with my wishes, and that those objects—persons, ideas, situations—"will become distorted under such coercion" as I may wish to exercise.

That distortion is an effect, or consequence, of the disordered will, which presses us to insist even where we know better than to do so. To insist that pain is always mental and can be ignored. That we are not jealous when we are jealous. Not faithless when we have no faith. Not weak or timid when we lack courage. The will declares that it is possible to admire what we do not admire and to love what we cannot love. It declares that we must be humble and forbearing when we know ourselves to be anything but. It insists—Farber's sly example—that we can achieve simultaneous orgasm at will even when repeated experience suggests to us that this is not routinely in our power. Again and again, at every point in our lives, we confront limitation, and our refusal to acknowledge that simple fact is at the root of problems many of us refuse to identify.

But there is a species of distortion that profoundly affects the way we think about ideas. We know all too well that an idea can seem compelling to us principally because we feel proud to own it. Not long ago many writers and intellectuals were invested in "derangement." To be committed to sanity and lucidity was by definition to cut oneself off from the most intense kinds of experience, to allow the fear of flying to disastrously limit our prospects. Derived from figures such as Dostoyevsky and Baudelaire, Bataille and Burroughs, "derangement" marked for generations of intellectuals a liberation from reasonableness and the settled bourgeois life of compromise and accommodation. The will to derangement took many different forms, from the use of drugs to the sophomoric posturings of persons determined to behave badly so as not to be regarded as conformist or genteel. In most cases, the will to derangement was not accompanied by any actual intention to go mad or to renounce the milder satisfactions. The acting out intended to signify liberation was in many cases the expression of a conformism as pronounced as the conformism of most other well-adjusted bourgeois adults. What could not be willed, in spite of the widespread will to derangement, was the radical intransigence that entails a genuine resistance to fashion or ideology of any kind.

At the present moment the will to adopt what are felt to be the most advanced or high-minded ideas is rarely accompanied by any commensurate seriousness. Consider the commitment of so-called conservatives to ideas they hold sacred, ideas like "freedom," which is often invoked by conservatives as freedom from government intervention. A recent editorial in the right-wing magazine the *New Criterion*, by its editor Roger Kimball, cites as examples of ostensibly idiotic liberal interventionism the efforts to address "the putative exhaustion of the world's resources," the determination to do something about "giant automobiles" or "disposable packages and containers," and efforts to address third-world poverty and global warming. So total is the will to mock and resist any form of government intervention that there can be no allowance for the possibility that the problems targeted in the initiatives Kimball names can have any legitimate claim on our attention. Here we have an instance of the conservative will attempting to do the work of the imagination. Which imagination? The one that would permit even a marginally thoughtful person to acknowledge the existence of actual problems that compel our decent attention. And thus it is astonishing, not that a reputable conservative "thinker" should deride the efforts or strategies of "liberals" to accomplish their ends, but that the ends themselves—from control of global warming to the amelioration of poverty—should themselves seem unreal and ridiculous. Anyone doubtful about the degree to which the will can more or less wholly incapacitate an entire generation of "principled" persons need only study the efforts of contemporary American conservatives to will away much that is indisputably real in our common experience.

But in some respects the more disappointing spectacle is presented by the efforts of liberal academics and intellectuals to deny what is entailed in the ideas to which they are attached. A few years ago I found myself seated next to a professor from a nearby college, much like my own small liberal arts college. Friendly, garrulous, confiding, the fellow soon began chattering about his students, how much he liked them, in spite of the fact that a good many of them were "detached" and expected to do well simply by showing up. And so, I then asked him, do you give out lots of low grades? Oh, no, he said. I don't do low grades. No need for that. And so how do you explain to the students the weight you will accord to exams? Oh, but I don't give exams, never have, never will, he said. Don't believe in them or in teaching to tests. At which point I felt I understood what I was confronting, which is to say, a nice man, no doubt, or probably so, a first-rate student himself, once upon a time, but not—so I felt—at all disposed to seriously examine his own ostensibly advanced assumptions. This impression I confirmed in the ten or fifteen further minutes of our peaceful, comradely exchange, in which, I might add, this somewhat younger man, sporting a ponytail somewhat fuller than my own, displayed no inclination to ask me about my own pedagogy, and just as well.

I cite this trivial exchange because it exhibits another aspect of the phenomenon that continues to puzzle me. My companion was, after all, a fellow with a few more or less plausible ideas he had taught himself to believe in, ideas he was open and comfortable about. Ideas few academics of his acquaintance would be likely to challenge or dismiss, whatever their own pedagogic practice. One was that it isn't good to teach to the test, another that tests don't reveal everything a student knows or doesn't know, and that in any case, as the fellow said, there are different kinds of knowledge. Interesting, I said—using a word I often use when students come out with an earnest banality—and left it at that.

Again, as I say, trivial, all of it, and yet telling, in that my companion had the will to proclaim his adherence to a few currently fashionable notions that attested—so he felt—to his status as an independent thinker who had advanced beyond the ordinary professor's acceptance of standardized tests and grading protocols and other traditional devices. I have no interest, not here, at any rate, in making a case for exams. But I am interested in the distortions entailed in the way our professor related to ideas. Remember, this was a guy whose students were, by his own account, not exactly lit up by the books they were reading or the instruction he was dispensing at the selective liberal arts college he taught at. His policies were clearly unproductive. Failures. Of course he had no way of ascertaining how little his students were learning, though he could tell that most of them were disengaged. His principled refusal—he himself thought of it as principled—to test them had not, clearly, encouraged them to embrace learning for its own sake. His cheerful, unchastened benevolence had solely to do with his will not to disappoint himself by violating a couple of ideas he had long ago talked himself into.

Of course the logic informing this man's thinking might instead have led him to the conclusion that his disinclination to give out low grades would be a violation of other principles. After all, he took himself to be a man of principle, and as such it might have occurred to him that he had a responsibility to assess his students, one way or another, the better to urge them to improve both their work and their attitudes toward study. Thus, for example, he might have decided to sit each student down for an hour or more of conversation at the close of each semester, so as to gain some modest foundation for an end-of-term assessment. But no, here was a fellow whose will would not allow such an alternative, given that mere conversation would inevitably fail to show *everything* a student knew. Better, in the estimation of this man of principle, simply to hand out high grades even if students had apparently, by his own estimation, done nothing to earn them.

My companion was thus in the grip of a delusion fostered by his efforts to will what could not be willed. He could not will a satisfactory outcome for students who might actually have learned something from him. Neither could he will a decent account of his own pedagogy, which was indisputably a failure, however mildly he registered that outcome. Nor could he will a compelling account of the thing that meant the most to him, which was his own virtue, given that he could feel principled and virtuous only by refusing to take seriously what was actually entailed in his complacently unrigorous stance.

No need here to get into the kind of research, widely publicized even in daily newspapers and weekly magazines, that explains that students who prepare for tests are more likely to master course materials than those who face no exams, or that when students actually take exams, and write elaborate responses to essay questions, they hold on to what they have learned much more securely than students without that experience. The point, for our purposes, is simply that a fellow like my fond companion might well have taken such research into account, but that the will to operate in terms of principles that flattered his sense of himself as advanced and non-traditional insulated him from any kind of serious thinking. Here was a man with the cheerful bonhomous demeanor of someone accustomed to living without conflict, in the safe company of the like-minded.

Here was a man with the cheerful bonhomous demeanor of someone accustomed to living in the company of the like-minded.

The failure to acknowledge our all-too-common subordination to the disordered will is striking and pervasive. In a new edition of his book *The Reckless Mind*, Mark Lilla notes "the countless cases of intellectuals whose political commitments did not pervert their thinking." But he also notes a great many instances in which reputable thinkers have been seduced by ill-digested ideas that have led them to deny the obvious, or to refuse to so much as consider what may be entailed in their principles or avowals. "The militancy of his nostalgia is what makes the reactionary a distinctly modern figure," Lilla writes, and of course it is the "militancy" with which other sentiments are sometimes held that accounts for a bizarre enlistment in the service of willfulness and denial.

In my own college department I was recently involved, as a committee member, in the search to hire a full-time fiction writer. From more than two hundred applicants we brought to campus four finalists, each of whom went through a day of meetings with twenty-five department members, assorted students, and deans. At 5 p.m., each candidate gave a demonstration class to a half dozen students and fielded questions from faculty members seated as onlookers at the back of the classroom. In the course of his half hour taking questions, one of our finalists, thinking, no doubt, to impress us, called some of the questioners by their first names—Bob, April, and so on. But this proved to be disastrous, in that our brilliant young novelist confused the first names of two persons, the only two Asian-American faculty in the department. Neither of them corrected him, and of course it was clear that the writer had no notion of the grave sin he had committed.

At a meeting of the department a week later, the department chair apologized to us all for failing to intervene at that critical juncture and in effect put us on notice, unmistakably, that, so far as she was concerned, the writer's candidacy was dead in the proverbial water.

Is this a little story about the operation of will? In truth it reveals several things about where we are at this moment in the culture.

But for now, let us think about it without straying too far from the relevant facts of the story. Thus, a person in a highly charged moment, after a long day of meeting thirty-five people he has never met before, makes a mistake. The mistake reveals one thing we can be certain about: that he was guilty of an error in judgment when he decided to try to call people by their names. Might the error have revealed something more? Possibly yes, possibly no. Was the error a sufficient reason to disqualify him? Did the confusion about the names of two Asian-American faculty expose the man as a "racist"? Say, rather, that the determination to disqualify him from further consideration was powered by the collective will to certify that such an error is never to be tolerated or forgiven. Neither is anyone permitted to acknowledge that sometimes a mistake is just a mistake, that we are all susceptible to making such mistakes, or that judgments based upon insufficient evidence of malice or callous indifference are not to be trusted.

The recent incident called to mind another encounter. Two years earlier I had appeared at a Bard College conference sponsored by the Hannah Arendt Center, where I served as one of two respondents to Claudia Rankine, whose National Book Critics Circle Award–winning book *Citizen* I had taught in a graduate course at the New School for Social Research. In my response to the book I spoke briefly about an especially memorable anecdote. A close friend of the author called her "by the name of her black housekeeper," so that the friend is said to have perhaps thought that "all black people look alike." Though Rankine informs us that she "never called her [friend] on it," and wonders why not, she doesn't quite provide an answer. In my response I speculated that the answer seemed to the poet obvious and indisputable: that white people, including the author's close friends, are often disappointing (fair enough) and that black people are so often on the receiving end of insults and aggressions—intentional or unintentional—that there is nothing new to say on that score (again, fair enough).

But then I also suggested that perhaps there is always more to say, especially where friends are involved, or where we lack sufficient evidence to convict someone of an unforgivable offense. Here, again, it seemed to me, the will to insist upon a definite, unimpeachable reading of an incident—which might well have been read in other, more generous ways—was a mark of a bewildering denial: a denial of the imagination that, liberated to do its proper work, can lead us in alternative directions.

But my story has one further component. I had met Claudia Rankine for the first time about fifteen minutes before we went on stage together in front of a large audience. We chatted a bit, noted that we had friends in common, and spoke also with the two other participants: a younger woman on the Bard College faculty and our chair, Roger Berkowitz, director of the Arendt Center. After Rankine's reading from *Citizen*, and the two formal responses, Rankine moved to the lectern and spoke, with characteristic eloquence and candor, about our remarks on her book. Throughout she referred to me as Roger, five or six times, and then again several times when we were all taking audience questions. This seemed to me not at all disturbing or insulting. The audience had come to Bard not to see me but to listen to Rankine, who had earlier professed some feeling for my magazine, *Salmagundi*, but clearly knew rather little about me or my work. The audience members had a program with my name correctly indicated, and none of what had transpired seemed to me a big deal. I admire Rankine, while disagreeing with several things she says in her book, and at the end of our panel, when we stood together on stage, she said that the session had gone well, and that perhaps we might think of taking our little show "on the road."

But then we saw, streaming toward the stairs on both ends of the elevated stage, more than a hundred people, all carrying copies of *Citizen* that they hoped to have signed. The first of those to reach us, huddled around the lectern, were two middle-age women, who at once scolded Rankine for calling me Roger, and thereby confusing the names of "the two white men on the stage." "And you," they went on, "are someone who knows how hurtful that can be, and talk so much about that very thing in your book. Don't you think you owe this man an apology, right now, in front of everyone up here?" Of course Rankine was astonished at this, and repeated, several times, "Did I really do that?" before I could bring out my own words, repeating, several times, that I wanted no apology, needed none, and that sometimes a mistake is just a mistake.

A half hour or so later, when Rankine had signed all the books, and was hurried away to another appearance by her agent, she called to me, across the aisles and rows, in a booming voice, Robert, Robert, Robert, Robert. And we both laughed, and that was that.

Now I don't at all wish to use any part of my story to make a case about what is and is not entailed when names are confused, or when someone's true sentiments are revealed, or obscured, by an error. But I do want at least to indicate that when we are not utterly in the iron grip of the will, it is possible to acknowledge the several dimensions of an encounter, and thus to respond without recourse to posturing and the peremptory dismissal of ordinary fellow-feeling and forgiveness.

None of us can hope to be fully exempt from distortions of will. We see the operation of willfulness and denial even in writers or thinkers whose work we otherwise admire. I remember well my own attraction to the work of Herbert Marcuse, who became something of a guru figure to people of my own left generation in the 1960s. Of course there were good reasons to be attracted to Marcuse, whose seminal books, from *Eros and Civilization* to *One-Dimensional Man*, introduced many Americans to "negative dialectic" and other heady theories associated with the Frankfurt School.* And I remember too the romantic notions inspired in us by our acquaintance with thinkers—especially Theodor Adorno and Walter Benjamin—who, like Marcuse, fled Nazi Germany and whose works made American pragmatist thinking seem timid and conventional.

The romance was sufficient to win us to ideas that might have seemed, even to young inebriates like me, somewhat misguided. Thrilling, of course, to dwell on the "false consciousness" that afflicted just about everyone in so-called open societies like our own, and of course we panted for ever more audacious assertions in the brief Marcuse was building against "the bourgeois democratic order." And thus were we much taken with Marcuse's assault on "Repressive Tolerance," in which he argued—as Alasdair MacIntyre explained—that because most of us are "effectively controlled by the system" and cannot really grasp what is being done to us, "freedom of speech is not an overriding good, for to allow freedom of speech in the present society is to assist in the propagation of error." All that we can hope for, Marcuse argued, is that we will be "reeducated into the truth" by an enlightened minority, "who are entitled to suppress rival and harmful opinions." Needless to say, Marcuse took himself to be a member of that elite minority, and people like me, who had the good sense to approve of his views, were likewise

---

* This school originated in Germany in 1923 and was really more of an intellectual movement than a brick-and-mortar operation. When several of its leading proponents came to the United States in the 1930s and 1940s, the movement became famous for its promotion of "critical theory" and its sustained examination of ideology and mass culture.

entitled to think of ourselves as among the happy few. Really, who would not thrill to such an idea when so much was at stake, and when our virtue was guaranteed by embracing a program so obviously bold and so at odds with our own former ideals of liberal tolerance, which it pained us—so we told ourselves—to renounce.

I remember well the exertion of will required for a guy like me to remain invested in this notion of repressive tolerance, and remember too the reluctance with which I let go of it when I saw that I myself had come to embody the will trying to do the work of the imagination. For I had not allowed myself to imagine the absurdity of the idea I had committed to, the comical self-importance of the posture entailed in holding that I and my comrades were an elite magically set apart from others and somehow immune to the false consciousness to which those others had succumbed. By the time I read MacIntyre's devastating critique of Marcuse in early 1971, I had come, on my own, to draw back a bit from Marcuse's argument, but MacIntyre's succinct dismissal decisively helped me through. "It is a necessary condition of rationality," I read, "that a man shall formulate his beliefs in such a way that it is clear what evidence would be evidence *against* them and that he shall lay himself open to criticism and refutation . . . But to foreclose on tolerance is precisely to cut oneself off from such criticism and refutation. It is gravely to endanger one's own rationality by not admitting one's own fallibility."

Thus I had failed, for a while, at least, to consider how vulnerable Marcuse and his followers were to delusion, buying into an "advanced" idea by refusing to imagine what would follow should the idea actually be adopted by persons with some power to make it effectual. The air of omniscience that attends the will to power of persons who have no misgivings about their membership in a benevolent ideological vanguard is of course much in evidence

WILLING WHAT CANNOT BE WILLED

today, and I am grateful to look back on my own delirious moment as a sort of cautionary tale about the ways of the will.

It does bear repeating, though, that the disordering at issue here has been notable even in the thinking of persons many of us admire. No less a scholar than Edward Said taught us to take seriously the idea known as blaming the victim, an idea now widely popular in ways that seemed improbable even to Said. For him the idea was especially compelling in the Middle East, where it had been customary for decades to blame Palestinians, routinely referred to as "terrorists," for the abject failure of the so-called peace process, which many of us hoped would conclude with the withdrawal of Israelis from the occupied territories seized in the 1967 Six-Day War. Thus "blaming the victim" was an idea rooted in a particular time and place, and its application to other places and times could only be problematic, though by no means dismissible. Even in the case Said invoked, there was reason to ask whether either party to the dispute had an exclusive claim on the status of "victim," and whether it is reasonable, in an ongoing debate, to suppress criticism of people who have suffered. In academic circles influenced by Said, any reference to acts of "terrorism" was soon regarded as off-limits, a reflection of Zionist efforts to discredit the legitimate aspirations of a subject population by casting aspersions on their so-called freedom fighters. In this way, "blaming the victim" was deployed as an ideological weapon that might constrain debate.

By now "blaming the victim" has taken a heavy toll on our efforts to speak honestly about many burning issues. In recent years, the idea has been embraced by people determined not to offend others or to hurt their feelings. This determination has become a peculiar feature of American life, peculiar in that the will not to offend is regarded as having nothing to do with censorship or, more emphatically, with the kind of self-censorship that forbids people to entertain even thoughts that seem to them genuinely compelling. The characterization of entire groups as victims has underwritten the conviction that such groups may never be subjected to criticism of any kind. Those of us who think to raise troubling questions about the fanaticism and cruelty of Jewish settlers in the occupied territories of the West Bank and thereby to raise questions about the rapidly changing character of Israeli society are told to cease and desist. Just so, to want to talk about the assault on enlightenment values carried on by imams in Dutch or Parisian mosques is felt to be anti-Islamic and thus indecent.

The will required to uphold the proscription against blaming the victim is considerable. It entails, after all, a strictly managed effort not to acknowledge things that may threaten our principled benevolence. The refusal to acknowledge the obvious extends to the element of condescension. For what can be more condescending than the thought that other persons are incapable of handling criticism or benefiting from the free play of ideas? Do we not thereby deny to those we would protect the intellectual courage they might summon to engage their critics? In doing so, of course, we will what cannot be willed: first, that our condescension nowhere be acknowledged or felt as such; and second, that persons condescended to will be grateful and thus respond in the way that the cadres of the right-minded would hope. Has Israeli behavior toward its subject population notably improved as a result of efforts to constrain criticism of Israeli policy in American political circles? Clearly not. Is there evidence of significant improvement in the quality of the political discourse in most Islamic countries as a result of strenuous Western efforts not to dwell too insistently on distressing and inconvenient matters—such as the fact, noted by Slavoj Žižek, that in such countries "there is no respect . . . for other people and their religion—a respect that is demanded from the West"? Again, clearly not. A fact not widely acknowledged, like many others, including what Žižek calls "the brutal and vulgar anti-Semitic and anti-Christian caricatures that abound in the press and schoolbooks of Muslim countries."

But then, honest writers like Žižek, and the late Oriana Fallaci, know very well that most enlightened persons in the West regard such observations as distasteful and do their best not to notice them, building around themselves a wall of denial. Better, apparently, as one prominent journalist named Carla Power suggests, to accentuate the positive and to think instead of "how much we share with Muslims," even when we might also acknowledge that there is much we do not share. In truth, of course, though we trumpet our respect for difference, we are much of the time unnerved by differences that are more than skin-deep.

No doubt we can hope to grow out of the delusions and denials to which we are variously susceptible. I have long been moved by Rosa Luxemburg's assertion that "freedom is always the freedom to think otherwise," and thus I've been attracted to contrarians, to people whose instinct is to go against the grain of officially accredited views—especially those accredited within their own circle of progressive thinkers. This has its dangers, to be sure. And yet I trust this instinct more than any other, simply because it is unlikely to allow for the species of self-approval that comes from embracing ideas most likely to be approved by others. Oscar Wilde and Groucho Marx were both onto something when they noted that they would prefer not to belong to any club that would have them. That goes, so far as I am concerned, even for the club of the healthy-minded left liberals in which most of my friends and familiars abide.

The will, then, especially the will to belong, is a peculiar faculty, which has its way with us more than we think, and drives us to seek the status of the saved, of those who know themselves to be in the right and deny anything that might interfere with their stern rectitude. Everywhere I discover that good people are inclined to frame arguments so as to avoid disappointing their own constituencies. At a lecture, a distinguished classicist argues that the Western attack on honor killings in Islamic societies betrays what she calls "entirely insidious motives." What can she mean? She is quite clear on this: such attacks, she argues, are "a way of attacking immigrant communities and encouraging racial hatred." Shut up, chatterboxes, is the unmistakable message here. Just keep those thoughts to yourselves. Be nice.

Precisely these kinds of arguments are at the core of efforts to constrain debate on the situation of black America. Ta-Nehisi Coates has been out front and influential in this, as where he mocks educators who would speak of "'personal responsibility' in a country authored and sustained by a criminal irresponsibility." The message, fully explicit, that if you accede to the words—I, for one, reluctantly accede to them—"in a country authored and sustained by a criminal irresponsibility" you will then of course agree not to talk about anything inconvenient that looks at all like blaming the victim.

For many of those who came of age in the 1960s, a first introduction to the phenomenon I have been describing was provided by the publication of Hannah Arendt's *Eichmann in Jerusalem*, which inspired a barrage of furious disparagement. Most of the outrage was focused on the relatively few pages Arendt devoted to the complicity of her fellow Jews in facilitating "the final solution." Though this was by no means Arendt's primary purpose, her critics insisted that it was her obligation to stick to the crimes committed by the Nazis and to avoid creating confusion about the relative status of victims and perpetrators. This line of argument has persisted into the present moment, wherever the work of Arendt is studied and debated. Out of bounds, it is said, are the efforts of that "self-hating Jew" to examine the work of the Jewish Councils, whose members cooperated with the Nazis in the hope that they might somehow do some good, buy some time, even save what they called "extraordinary persons" in return for assembling the names and whereabouts of other not-so-extraordinary Jews. In arguing that, without the efforts of the Councils, the Nazis would not have been able to kill so many Jews, Arendt opened up questions that are regarded even now as distasteful, offensive, and therefore unacceptable.

My point here is not that Arendt made no errors in her book, nor that the assertions she made about the Jewish Councils were indisputably accurate. Arendt was writing about issues of enormous complexity and moral urgency, and she had to know that much of what she said would be disputed. But she did not anticipate the efforts to censure her for raising legitimate questions. In her book she tried to anticipate and to answer the kinds of objections likely to come from thinkers like Martin Buber and Gershom Scholem, who did indeed, vigorously, relentlessly, attack what she had written. Fair enough. But it should have been clear even to her most vehement critics that she had written in good faith. At the end of her book she imagined what her own decision to sentence Eichmann to death—in her own terms, for her own reasons, according to her own carefully articulated logic—would sound like to others like Buber who opposed that conclusion. And she imagined, again and again, what the facts she recited might imply about the rest of us, asking how long it would take for the average person to become a criminal under extreme circumstances. Arendt's will to be true to the facts at her disposal and to the primary idea she developed about "the banality of evil" in no way entailed a resolve to deny inconvenient facts that contradicted the impression she hoped to convey.*

But good faith was not much in evidence in the efforts of many critics to rule out aspects of the case she mounted. This was the most discouraging and shocking aspect of the dispute that erupted around Arendt's book. For many readers, Arendt had violated her obligation not only to proceed with due caution but to refuse absolutely to introduce unsavory questions. It was one thing for Arendt to mock Eichmann or to recount the acts of sadists and corrupt officials or even to note the widespread Arab enthusiasm for Hitler. But it was another thing to indulge in a little sarcasm on the subject of rabbinic laws or to ask why more Jews did not resist the Nazis or to suggest that the "moral collapse" encompassed pretty much everyone, Nazis and Jews, victims and perpetrators. To venture into such territory—so a great many critics argued—was clearly a violation of common decency. The will not to imagine was at the root of the attack on Arendt, who was obliged not to wonder about the felt experience of persons involved in the Holocaust—not if that exercise of imagination might potentially open up questions that would seem to many of her readers deeply upsetting.

One more time: the will trying to do the work of the imagination. To preserve a fixed idea of what is legitimate and acceptable while pretending to think.

---

* In a recent book on Zionism and the political Left (*The Lion's Den*), Susie Linfield contends that Arendt's language prompted the visceral reactions to *Eichmann in Jerusalem*: "Cleverly, slyly," Linfield writes, "she takes ordinary words and phrases that are loaded with historical meanings and twists them in perverse ways" clearly designed to act on readers—especially Jewish readers—"like little knife wounds to the gut." Among the terms anatomized by Linfield are "show trials" and "selections," terms calling to mind the worst aspects of terror regimes, thereby linking them, "either explicitly or by implication, with the Zionist movement" and the trial of Eichmann itself. Much though I am persuaded by Linfield's account of Arendt, I find nothing "perverse" in Arendt's language, which seems to me precise and appropriately disturbing.

THE IDENTITY TRAP

How to define "provincialism"? As the inability (or the refusal) to see one's own culture in the large context.

—Milan Kundera

Making political claims that are based on identity is what white supremacy is.

—Jill Lepore

A psychoanalyst friend tells me he despairs when a patient announces, in the course of a therapeutic session, that he doesn't do this, never does that. Doesn't. Never. Can't. A way of deflecting what might otherwise have been a helpful suggestion, a strategy for warding off conflict or distress. Apology? Not what I do. Not in me. Occasional words of tenderness or encouragement? Not my way. Some willingness to bend in argument? Not who I am. Wouldn't know how.

That sense of a fixed disposition, rooted in a deep conviction of what is and is not possible, describes a version of identity to which a great many of us subscribe. When I say that I am not a man who cheats on his wife, I am citing more than a fact. I am naming what I take to be a constitutive element of my very being, an element without which I would not know who I am. When I say that I am allergic to what passes for spirituality among persons who wear their religious sentiments on their outsize sleeves, I am confirming an aspect of my identity apt to be entirely familiar to my family and friends. The words "doesn't do this, never does that"—however much I may deplore them—do in fact reflect my sense of myself as a person with limitations and affiliations, tendencies and aversions. I may like—some of the time, at least—to think of myself as a man eminently unpredictable and open, susceptible to the widest possible range of impulses and influences. Yet I know that really there are all sorts of things I won't, can't, wouldn't do, and that what sets me apart from others with an even more settled disposition is merely my willingness to entertain misgivings about my own peculiar proclivities.

To many of us "identity" has long seemed a problem. Even those of us who feel that we know, more or less, who we are may well feel uneasy about aspects of our identity we have been loath to explore. Ought I to think about my own middle-class status when the story I have invented about myself and my work has never required that I pay much attention to class? Ought I to think, more than I am inclined to do, about the fact that I am white, when so far as I can tell whiteness has never been an important factor in the fashioning of my identity—whatever the advantages it has brought me? If I have left behind the religion of my fathers and not set foot in a Jewish temple in decades, must I routinely describe myself not only as a Jew but as a man whose current views of Israelis, Palestinians, anti-Semitism, and the "occupied territories" are largely determined by the fact that his grandfather was a rabbi? Am I not to be believed when I say that the word "male," like the epithet "predatory," does not begin to name what I take myself essentially to be?

We don't always get to decide what others see when they sum us up or reduce us to a caricature of the rich and various selves we think we have fashioned. One night, at a panel discussion in a packed college auditorium, an old friend, seated in the audience, raised her hand and admonished me for "pretending not to know very well what's meant by the term 'alpha males,'" when "in truth, Bob, the term describes you perfectly." Though taken aback, I managed to emit a nervous laugh, and at once conceded that I do shoot off my mouth rather more than I should and don't at all shy away from dispute. "Oh, but it's more than that," my friend shot back, "and you really ought to own up to it."

Of course I knew that an opening had now been cleared to talk about the theme to which a great many of my friends are inexorably drawn, the theme of power and the way it infects even our most ordinary relations with one another. But that was not the theme of our discussion that evening, and the reference to "alpha males" had been a casual aside dropped in by another speaker, so that I decided, on the spot, not to speak of "power," but to note that my friend was herself, by any reasonable standard, as much an "alpha" as her friend Bob, and that I have long numbered among my friends a wide assortment of powerful women—from

The theoretical climate of gender-inflected cut and thrust has left us with a stale remnant of increasingly empty ideas.

Susan Sontag to Mary Gordon and Carolyn Forché—who have taught me to believe that the term "alpha" ought really to be extended beyond its familiar application to the species "male." A trivial observation? Maybe. But it is, after all, the case that we tend, all of us, to grow too comfortable with categories that make of identity a baldly obvious and undifferentiated fact. The intensity and forthrightness of the "alpha" character are not invariably the mark of a uniquely male disposition, nor of the indomitable virus of superiority. Assertion, even self-assertion, does not invariably bespeak an urge to annihilate the opposition or to wield coercive power. The theoretical climate of gender-inflected cut and thrust has done its mostly beneficial work, but it has also left us with a stale remnant of received and increasingly empty ideas.

This is not at present the kind of argument that anyone can hope to win, but it does surely prompt speculation about our attraction to identity as a formula we think we can master, in spite of the fact that it is an idea notoriously subject to varieties of cant, delusion, and gross misuse. We do suspect, don't we, that so-called alpha males are often vulnerable and insecure persons whose bluster and self-confidence serve principally as a mask to cover over weakness? That apparently timid or reluctant persons often burn with a furious desire to leave a violent scar on the map? That persons shamelessly direct and brutally honest are some of the time inspired by hatred of injustice and love of the truth? We understand, do we not, that the seductive and promiscuous young are often in the vanguard of those most apt to charge others with advantage, predation, and varieties of "inappropriate" behavior? We are many things, never but one thing. Standard gender designations are unduly literal and inadequate. Takes it like a man? Cries like a girl? Sensitive like a woman? Who would any longer wish to rely on such formulas? We may want to resist the notion that gender is merely incidental to our identity, but we can surely agree that we are, each of us, a great deal more than our gender designation. The rage for "identity" too often bespeaks a preference for simplicity rather than for complexity.

That preference for simplicity is beautifully interrogated in a novel called *Open City* by Teju Cole, in which Julius, the young black narrator, navigates his experience and examines his own thoughts with astonishing delicacy. In one especially striking passage Julius encounters two young black men on a Harlem street and exchanges glances with them, establishing what he takes to be a "tenuous" but familiar kind of connection, the looks "a gesture of mutual respect based on our being young, black, male; based, in other words, on our being 'brothers.' These glances were exchanged between black men all over the city every minute of the day," Julius continues, "a quick solidarity worked into the weave of each man's mundane pursuits. . . . It was a little way of saying, I know something of what life is like for you out here."

Of course you take this in and you think, by all means, "brothers," bound into a "quick solidarity" by glances certifying that "we" share a knowledge and a set of expectations that others outside our condition, our identity, cannot share. And yet within a page of the passage certifying that shared identity, the two strangers begin a violent assault on their young black brother, a Nigerian doctor who in truth has rather less of a "connection" to the perpetrators than he had supposed, the two young black men, joined by a third, relentless in their brutalization of this "brother," whose temperament and endowments have made him a person not remotely inclined to the "violence for sport" that marks the identity of his assailants and others like them. The obvious marks of identity in this case, as in most others, are unreliable. In some ways, the most reliable marker differentiating the Nigerian doctor from his assailants is the fact that, in his pain and anger, "every cliché by which the assault could be minimized hurried to claim space in [his] head." Identity here not a matter of ethnicity or of a spurious "solidarity" which was, surely in this case, delusional. What, we ask, do we really know when we think we know?

The English painter Lucian Freud was best known for portraits that interrogate his subjects and provide what one writer called "the means to register [their] specificity." But that specificity is by no means a gateway to a secure grasp of a sitter's identity. Even when Freud's subjects have names and identifiable faces and signifying accoutrements—the crown on the head of Queen Elizabeth, the riding crop in the hand of an equestrian, the brush in the hand of a painter—identity remains decidedly out of reach, the pronounced expression, even on an especially expressive countenance, often misleading, never defining. The naked woman lying faceup on a mattress, reddened eyes staring helplessly up at the painter, might well be taken for his victim or subordinate, a poor pathetic wretch, when in fact her status and actual identity are no more knowable than those belonging to dozens of other such models captured by Freud in just such a posture—models who included his own lovers, wives, and children. We look, we study, we presume, and find that we know not nearly what we presume to know. I think about the identity of Lucian Freud himself, say that he was fierce and pitiless, that I can see in his work the unmistakable signs of an identity belonging to a man who had no use for the pieties or sentimentalities, who used—used up—women, especially women, with the feral abandon of a satyr. And yet the testimony of friends and children substantially complicates the portrait and our sense of what we see in the brutally frank paintings he made.

Of course intimate acquaintance with an actual person will usually provide a more persuasive—though often mistaken—impression of identity than a painted portrait. When I look at my wife I see many things that even Lucian Freud would not have been able to show. And still I am certain, after forty-five years of marriage, that in signal respects she remains somewhat unfathomable, both to me and to herself.

Not all of us will think the identity question so very important. It may be that Lucian Freud would have considered it irrelevant and a bore. Why not? Like other such preoccupations, it can seem irresistible or absurd, an urgent injunction to "know thyself" or a lure promising only self-deception. On a recent winter evening a student stopped me on a New York City sidewalk, just outside The New School for Social Research, and asked if I had ever met James Baldwin, whose work she was reading for the first time in a graduate course I was teaching that semester. Only once, I told her, promising more but rushing off to catch a late-night train, and then, stirred by her question, musing for hours about Baldwin's arduous interrogation of identity. No doubt whatsoever: Baldwin did not think of identity as irrelevant or boring. As a young man, after all, he went to France to avoid "becoming merely a Negro; or, even, merely a Negro writer." Though ever in pursuit of authenticity, he knew that it was a grave error to settle into what has been called the "idolatry of origins." Ambivalent about everything, he hated the idea of being reduced to a spokesman for his race. A recent biographer entitles his book *All Those Strangers* and identifies them as "Baldwin the deviant rabble rouser . . . ; Baldwin the civil rights activist . . . ; Baldwin the passé novelist and homosexual sidelined by Black Nationalists; Baldwin the expatriate; and the Baldwin struggling to work out his conflicted relationship to Africa."

But these terms only begin to get at "all those strangers" jostling for primacy in Baldwin, whose essays reveal him also to have been a passionate friend, a sometimes harsh and unforgiving critic even of persons who admired him, and a man who never successfully worked through unresolved conflicts with his own bitter father or a variety of other father figures. The Baldwin I met at a reception at the Village Gate nightclub in New York City in 1965, a few days after he returned from a long sojourn in Paris, was a generous and sweet-spirited man, so far as I could tell, the accent of grievance and rue very much in abeyance, moving as he did among people who had gathered to welcome him home. Of course Baldwin was always interrogating his sense of self, understanding as he did that he moved in what the philosopher Charles Taylor once called "a certain space of questions," identity never stable but subject to revision. In my one brief exchange with Baldwin I told him that my students—I was then teaching at a New York City public high school—were confused and disappointed by a sentence in which he declares that he never met a Negro who did not hate Jews. "Tell them," he said, a wide smile on his face, "not to believe everything they read." By no means the response of a defiantly embattled man determined, as he was, to lead a very public life in history. More determined—so I thought—to vacate or sidestep, where possible, the persona he had embraced.*

---

* The essayist Thomas Chatterton Williams has lately had much to say about the addiction to binary thinking in discussions of identity: "Indeed, to be black (or *white*) for any significant amount of time in America is fundamentally to occupy a position on the mongrel spectrum—strict binaries have always failed spectacularly to contain this elementary truth." Elsewhere, in the same essay ("Black and Blue and Blond"), Williams writes: "What I do know is that I used to not just tolerate but submit to and even on some deep level *need* our society's dangerous assumptions about race, even as I suspected them to be irredeemably flawed." That need kept him, he says, from relating even to his own family members "as distinct and irreplaceable people, not bodies or avatars or sites of racial characteristics and traits."

Identity is bound to seem especially urgent to those who live under the threat of prejudice, violence, or disapproval. A devout Muslim woman in a European country that has forbidden her to wear a headscarf will necessarily be consumed by questions of identity in a society that regards her as an outlier or a menace. Others, alert to a long history of oppression or prejudice, will cling to their own fiercely contested identity, refusing to be contaminated by contact with others. In certain neighborhoods of Brooklyn dominated by Orthodox Jews, my writer friend Steve Stern and his partner, Sabrina Jones, clad in jeans and T-shirts, riding their bicycles on a warm spring day, have been spat at by residents of the area who resent the "inappropriate" clothing they wear and their "nerve" in invading a district where they are clearly unwelcome. On a Paris street late one night, emerging from a Moroccan restaurant with the poet C. K. Williams and his family—who lived nearby—my wife, our teenage son, and I were violently abused and threatened by a man who had overheard us speaking in English and informed us— waving a metal trash can in our direction—that these were streets on which only Islamic people were permitted to walk. Identity, for people inflamed with the higher significance of their ethnicity and their sacred enclave, can be a fighting matter, and not at all a subject for polite conversation.

But then, even persons very much at home in a multiethnic and spectacularly diverse society may also find identity to be charged with significance beyond what some of us have ever experienced. My own son Gabe and my son-in-law, Drew, married and resident in Boston for a decade, both of them established figures in the cultural life of the city, are by no means reluctant to speak of the alternative benefits of time spent with other gay friends in notably gay enclaves like Provincetown. They tell me, in fact, what I have no reason to doubt, that to be gay is to have a relationship to identity that a straight white man like myself can but barely understand, in that I have never had to be aware of myself in a comparable way. Never had to think about whether or not it will seem offensive to others strolling along a sidewalk if I hold my wife's hand or, seated at a café, impulsively plant a kiss on her lips. Never had to wonder whether some flamboyance of dress or gesture will make others somehow uncomfortable and thus wish to escape my presence. Small things, perhaps, and yet belonging, as Gabe and Drew speak of them, to a wider range of felt deficits, impairments, or provocations that will tend to make their possessors wish to dig in their heels and lay claim to their special identity as if above all things it defined them.

But of course it doesn't define you, not really, is what, more or less, I have said in reply, whenever we have had that conversation. Oh, but it does, they assure me. More than you know. And however reluctantly, I have come to believe them, in spite of my long-held conviction that because we are many things, made up of so many different and often competing—even incompatible—endowments, we cannot possibly be defined by any one element of our disposition. That conviction is deep in me, one component of a liberal politics that admonished us, first as children, then as adults, not to judge people by the color of their skin or their gender or their religious or sexual orientation. Familiar stuff. Clichés. The words "not to judge" signifying "not to reduce people to a single feature that may tell you virtually nothing about what they really are and what may be expected of them." When I read an essay on "the racialization of Islam" in the United States and find that of course Muslims in this country are of many different minds about virtually everything, including the dictates of their professed religion, I am confirmed, for the moment, and deplore, quite as I was taught to do, efforts to "racialize" Muslims by associating their ethnicity with a particular set of characteristics. To be sure, there are Muslims who want to be defined utterly by the one true fact they value above all others. But there are as well Muslims who value in themselves many different things and regard themselves as multicultural individuals who contain multitudes—the very thing, as has been rightly said, the tribalists fear.

Of course one thing is not like another, and there is nothing, perhaps, comparable to traditional "tribalism" in the disposition my son and son-in-law describe. And yet I wonder. Much as I have wondered, more than occasionally, about my own identification with a tribe called the New York Jewish Intellectuals, to which in several respects I indisputably belong, for better or worse, and whose defining characteristics I've been told I share: the tendency to secularism and disputation, the lingering but somewhat hopeless romance with socialism, the sense of a shared history with other once oppressed people, the conviction that modernism and liberalism are not inevitably or always incompatible, the willingness to live with the notion that we are at last a somewhat comical "herd of independent minds," and the instinct to mistrust and attack any suggestion of tribal loyalty or ideological purity. Can members of a tribe seriously set themselves, more than occasionally, against their own kind, and take heart from the frequency with which they furiously contend with one another on issues of consequence?

My tribe, such as it is, has long felt that our own commitment to what Lionel Trilling called "variousness" was an essential element of our collective identity, and that in itself has made us wonder at others inclined, as we ourselves were not, to a more particularistic version of identity. Why the wish to be, above all, one certain thing? Why the affinity for a particular origin or, for that matter, for other persons who share a particular sexual disposition? Why accordance with those who share one single feature of our vastly complex orientation? I would no sooner think of myself as bound to or defined by other white male heterosexuals—as if they had in common, all of them, similar views, emotions, tastes, ambitions, deficits—than I would think myself bound to or defined by other English professors or husbands or fathers. And so I continue to be surprised—in spite of the many cogent explanations I have been offered—by the fact that my son and son-in-law choose to think that being gay defines them in a way that differs from anything I have known in myself.*

How, then, does this work, this sense of somewhat tribal belonging, embraced, acknowledged, celebrated by people who continue to regard themselves as worldly, open, tolerant, and various? Does it go beyond a simple wish, now and then, to be with people with whom you feel you can be yourself, principally because you share something of vital importance? If it were nothing more than that it would seem not at all surprising. Banal, in fact. Who does not enjoy spending time with like-minded people or with people who share a background, a set of more or less common experiences, from

---

* Mark Dery, the biographer of the book artist Edward Gorey, somewhat resents the fact that Gorey was casual about his homosexual identity, and regards someone who can downplay his sexual orientation as "blithely entitled." And yet Dery also speculates that Gorey was perhaps onto something when he rejected "the whole business of constructing identity . . . around sexuality." Dery also quotes a friend of Gorey's, who tells the biographer that people like Gorey "just see it in a whole different way. Being gay is not the center of their lives. . . . Ted never struck me as closeted; he was just who he was." "That's the correct answer," writes Joan Acocella in a review of the Gorey biography. I wish I could be as sure as all that.

coming out to divorce, from small-town life to religious conversion or disillusionment? Nothing really "tribal" in any of that, surely, however pleasurable the bonds established in the course of such encounters. And not much either to speak of in the way of identity formation—is there?—where like-minded or otherwise affiliated people get together to enjoy one another's company. The merely pleasant and merely comfortable are not sufficient to warrant the presumption of anything so definite and defining as the identity we associate with a community of believers confirming for themselves what in their truest selves they are.

At a *Salmagundi* magazine conference on identity several years ago the poet Tom Healy opened up a heated discussion, arguing that, with the advent of gay marriage, gay families, "safe neighborhoods," and the prospect of "living comfortably inside the bourgeois legal and political system," queer identity has become notoriously problematic. Previously, Healy argued, there was "a sense that we were . . . an outsider group" and that "our difference was a place of creativity": "In the past my queer identity suggested a more fluid engagement with people of all kinds of races and classes," Healy noted, something only possible "when gay culture was largely hidden" and "people broke traditional boundaries of affiliation." In the present situation, in effect, "the whole idea of difference has changed," not only because we've moved "beyond binary ideas of male and female" but because it's hard not to be at least somewhat nostalgic for a time when "things used to be simpler" and a gay man did not have to confront the thought that "my queerness as an identity is evaporating."

Of course Tom Healy knows that he is free to embrace and espouse "queerness," insofar as it seems to him a viable mode of self-definition. That, oddly, is one aspect of the problem, in that he would like not to think of "being gay" as an elementary sort of thing, a mere "consumer choice." On the other hand, as he concedes, queerness may no longer be a fully viable ideal, and the tribal dimension that was once felt to be a constitutive element of queer identity may be impossible for Healy and others to sustain.

The biographer Ruth Franklin has suggested that, to make further sense of these issues, we might invoke Andrew Solomon's notion of "vertical" and "horizontal" identities. "The vertical identity," she says, comes from thinking of oneself as the product of particular parents and thus belonging to and feeling a part of their community "as if it were a part of our family." At present, she goes on, many of us—certainly those of us who wish to identify as "queer"—are inclined not to define ourselves in this way but to declare that "my identity is not yours, I'm creating an identity for myself that is totally separate from the identity of the people, of the family that I came from," so that "I have to choose to affiliate myself with another community, and to find a way to integrate all the multiplicities of identity that are or have been a part of me." That, Healy says, is what happens "when you're experiencing a crisis of identity [and] discover that your family is not your community."

What I hear, then, in the efforts of my son Gabe and my son-in-law, Drew, to assert an identity largely defined by the fact that they are gay is the wish to constitute for themselves a community that is somewhat distinct from their families of origin. In some respects— so I tell myself—this is not so very different from what most of us have done or tried to do. We might even say that it is our task to find ways to differentiate ourselves from our families and communities of origin while trying to remember where we come from and why, exactly, we have labored to free ourselves from unhealthy subordination to those families and their ways. More often than necessary, perhaps, I have emphasized—certainly to myself—the familial bonds I have labored to create with a wide and scattered tribe of admired friends whose presence, as a community, in my thoughts and practices, allows me to know who I am. Though I have never been in flight from my family of origin—working class, Jewish, scrappy, committed to what John Murray Cuddihy once called "the ordeal of civility"—I have long wished to foster another kind of community.

And yet in important respects I concede that what people like myself have done, or tried to do, is actually quite different from the efforts of persons who bear inside them a memory of oppression, ostracism, or threat. Reluctantly I remind myself, again and again, that this is so. Again, the instinct to defend and identify with one's own is likely to be strongest among those who feel that others are against them or wish, for whatever reasons, to shun or denigrate them. It's perhaps too easy for me to say that each of us is inclined, like everyone else, to draw close to those with whom we share inalienable bonds and, at the same time, to draw gradually away, so as to create more diverse and unpredictable identities. Though that project seems to me attractive, it may well read too much like a formula. Secular liberals, myself very much included, are perhaps unduly inclined to suppose that we are moving, inexorably, toward a universal goal, and that everyone will regard the prospect of moving beyond parochial attachments as self-evidently beneficial. Nor will we agree, all of us, that what Gabe and Drew describe has anything to do with a parochial attachment. In discussions of identity and identity formation, there is a danger in viewing communities based on specific affinities as if they were by definition exclusive or narrow. Informing my own resolutely liberal perspective on identity is the danger of what John Gray calls "belligerent progressivism," that is, the notion that there is a "single form of collective life" to which we will all one day aspire.

———

I used to think that there was an essential distinction to be made between what the philosopher Akeel Bilgrami calls "subjective" and "objective" versions of identity. To be sure, there is and will always be a gap between what I am to myself and what I am to others. Objectively, it may well be, I give my students every reason to believe that I am self-assured and committed to a professorial demeanor that allows for few traces of weakness, apology, or sentimentality. Objectively the man with a knife in his hand who threatened my wife on a bus headed up to a music school in Fiesole some years ago was a barely human creature who deserved what she hoped would be the just desserts awaiting him. The Islamic woman in a London suburb who wears a hijab and tells an interviewer that she has chosen to be a covered woman and has never felt pressured by her husband or her community to do what she would prefer not to is objectively a devout adult, not a victim of coercion, who deserves to make choices for herself. In such cases we suspect that there is more to the story than the objective profile allows, though we are inclined to settle for the obvious and primary fact in some cases more than in others. Identity, even when it is objectively ascertained, is a reflection of the views and dispositions of those making the assessment. I have little inclination to think of the knife-wielding cur on the Italian bus as more than the terrifying figure he cut. Objectively I am well satisfied to regard his identity as if it were an elementary and fathomable phenomenon.

Bilgrami rightly observes that there is always a tension between so-called objective and subjective views of identity, and most of us would surely agree that we have felt that tension. When I behold my sons, it is likely that, in spite of our long acquaintance and continuing intimacy, I will not view them quite as they view themselves. There is the face they wear, even at their mother and father's dinner table, and the face they confront in the mirror when they retire at night. Again, these are commonplace observations, and yet, with so much nonsense in the air, anything obvious or plausible you may think to say about identity may well have its uses. This is especially so in an age of identity politics that, as Bilgrami notes, "has elevated some characteristics—nationality, ethnicity, linguistic and religious allegiances—beyond anything warranted by or echoed in the actual moral-psychological economies of ordinary citizens." Hard not to suspect that much of what passes for enlightened talk on the subject of identity is predominantly political, that is, constructed to accord with a particular community's current notion of what is and is not acceptable.

Of course it may well be that many of us do in fact feel entirely represented by the elevation of particular characteristics. The primacy accorded to Islamic identity or black identity or gay identity, even white identity, may often have to do not primarily with calculations about power or politics but with a fear of the uncertainties and hard choices that come with modernity and the need to think. Subjectivity itself is not for all of us a welcome burden. Questions and quandaries are often settled by a recourse to definite ideas and assumptions. Even the brave and crusading radical voices at the forefront of a social justice movement—#MeToo, black power, gay liberation—will often be tempted away from the

complex insights that initially fueled the urgency and thus toward
the parochial identity formulas that leave us wondering how anything so very promising can have come to this. For every brilliant
feminist writer—Francine Prose, Katha Pollitt, Honor Moore—
making the case for a plausibly complex view of where we are in the
immediate aftermath of #MeToo, there are countless other voices
sowing pointless triumphalist rage and flattening our common view
of identity. Nor are those
other voices confined to
the blogosphere. In the *New
York Times* a writer named
Lindy West issues op-eds
featuring what she herself
calls "a blazing affirmation
of young womanhood,"
directed at the creation of

*Identity thinking lends itself,
often in extraordinary ways, to
delusion. . . . Why the wish to be,
above all, one certain thing?*

a brave new world in which at last we understand that "pretty
much all media" bear responsibility for making all "complicated"
women feel "crazy" and "ugly" and all "complicated" men feel like
"geniuses." Where that species of identity politics has the platform
to run amok it will not be easy to engage in serious conversation.

In some ways the notion of identity as a subjective matter pres-
ents fewer immediate difficulties. People in a culture like ours
ordinarily suppose that they are more or less free to think about
themselves as they wish. If they are not much given to misgiving
or sustained reflection they will casually opt for a view of themselves they can hang on to and adequately represent—at least to
themselves. Lindy West can tell herself (in 2018!) that she is a voice
in the wilderness fighting against "our culture's hostility toward
women's sexual pleasure," and I can tell myself that, elderly though

I am, I will not go quietly when all about me I hear sound and fury in what Susan Jacoby calls an "age of unreason." Better yet, as Jacoby reports, students at law schools in the United States can tell themselves that they are brave and enlightened souls protecting women from harm by mobilizing to stop their professors from teaching rape law, on the grounds that doing so will potentially trigger unpleasant thoughts. Subjectively, we have, all of us, ways to mount pictures of ourselves that are at best incomplete, and at worst, as Jacoby says, finding the "correct word," plainly "stupid." Identity thinking does lend itself, often in extraordinary ways, to delusion.

Bilgrami is not alone in noting that identity thinking is bound to reflect "the zeitgeist of a particular period," with its fixed or fluid but always potent "conceptual categories." Those categories are often "hidden from the exercise of our reflective self-understanding," so that I may not at all see the degree to which I remain in thrall not only to the radical postures I adopted in the 1960s when I was a war resister but to a distorted view of what should now be possible for right-minded people like myself to accomplish. Identity, after all, is very much an aspect of the self-understanding, or lack of self-understanding, required to go against the grain of an established consensus. Think of what American intellectuals in the 1930s must have told themselves about who they were and what they were able to accomplish when they persisted in believing that they would soon bring about a Marxist revolution and do away with capitalism for good and all. The conceptual categories now dominant among us tend rather to promote other kinds of delusion, such as the notion that we can think well of ourselves if we mobilize to protect others from having unwanted or disturbing thoughts. The warrant to regard our own subjective instincts—especially when we are in step with others who share those instincts—as more or less always beneficial is a mixed blessing. We want, after all, not to love things—instincts, acts, ideas—principally because they are ours. Because they confirm the image we have of ourselves. We want, or ought to want, not to love ourselves as if our ostensible motives—to be right, to be good, to be correct—guaranteed defensible outcomes.

The historian Jennifer Delton opened up our understanding of identity in unexpected ways a few years ago when she wrote about the emerging academic field of whiteness studies, which is principally focused on "the tension between African Americans and whites" and insists that things in our society would improve if whites understood that they are a "race," rather than regarding race as "something others have." As long as whiteness remains "invisible, or deniable," whiteness scholars argue, whites alone will enjoy "the privilege of being the unracialized norm," and the so-called color-blind society will be one in which "everyone is like them, which is to say individuals for whom race doesn't matter." In denying that whiteness matters—so the argument goes—whites are "denying the importance of all race," and denying as well the fact that their "success and achievements are due in large part to their race and the privileges it gives them."

Obviously there is much to say on every aspect of this argument, much to say about the very different observation that, though racism and racial advantage are real and persisting, whiteness really may have more to do with "ideology, economic opportunity, and social status" than about race per se. It is not transparently obvious at all that "race" is an especially helpful way to think about where we are, much though it cannot be conveniently ignored. Delton is not alone in pointing out that we may well have exhausted the beneficial possibilities for thinking of race as the centrally important factor in our present condition, however much we are moved to invoke the names of persons—Michael Brown, Eric Garner, others—who have recently been killed or abused precisely because they were black. The philosopher Kwame Anthony Appiah contends that "there is nothing in the world that can do all we ask race to do for us." The revolutionary black writer Frantz Fanon, a native of Martinique long associated with the Algerian National Liberation Front, whose books on race were vitally important to generations of freedom fighters, argued almost a half century ago that "negritude" was "a black mirage" and that "the Negro is not. Anymore than the white man." The American critic Gerald Early notes that we have asked "race to do more work, support more of a psychological burden, than such a limited concept could ever hope to do."

When Delton argues that there are good reasons for whites not to think of themselves primarily as whites, she is operating within a framework established by generations of antiracist thinkers and activists who "sought to lessen the hold of 'race' over our society"—thinkers like "Franz Boas, Margaret Mead, Ruth Benedict, Melville Herskovits, and many others [who] tried to teach white Americans that 'race' was a social construction, a myth, a fallacy, a fiction." Though it suits those who want to make of identity a weapon in a war that pits oppressors against victims, race is not only an unfortunate emphasis but pernicious in a whole host of ways. As Ian Buruma writes, "identity, more and more, rests on the pseudoreligion of victimhood," at a time when most of us really find that there is "little Otherness left to defend" and older notions of identity, rooted in race or ethnic custom, no longer seem viable.

Appiah says of Americans, including black Americans, that "Their middle-class descendants, whose domestic lives are conducted in English and extend eclectically from *Seinfeld* to Chinese take-out, are discomfited by a sense that their identities are shallow by comparison with those of their grandparents, and some of them fear that unless the rest of us acknowledge the importance of their difference, there soon won't be anything worth acknowledging." Whiteness scholars have invested in those fears and in the fallacy of race as a primary fact we can do nothing but embrace and employ.

There is an odd but unmistakable element of determinism in this perspective, an element somewhat bizarre in a culture heavily invested in the idea of "choice." Many of us are prepared to believe that choice belongs among the most sacred of our entitlements, and even to declare it a natural right, associating it with justice itself, as if we were defined, both as a species and as an enlightened citizenry, by the exercise of choice. Strange, then, that even among many of those for whom "choice" is a fighting term, the inclination to suppose that we must uphold long-discredited notions about race and ethnicity remains strong, even where inconsistent. A colleague of mine who has done scholarly work in whiteness studies was surprised when I asked him one evening after a lecture whether he believes that Italians are more susceptible to misdemeanors, from petty malfeasance to genuinely corrupt behavior, than Americans. Why would you ask such a question? he replied, clearly taken aback by my apparently not-so-innocent question. Because, I told him, I had just read a provocative essay by Tim Parks, explaining that for all of his grotesque behavior, Silvio Berlusconi was still admired by most Italians, for whom the man's extravagant wheeling and dealing made their own smaller misdemeanors seem insignificant—this in a country with the highest rate of tax evasion in Europe and with other comparable stains on its public record. Why not, then, think about Italians as an ethnic group with characteristic tendencies, much in the way that many ostensibly enlightened persons are prepared to think about the characteristic tendencies of whites or males, the way men (and often women) used to speak openly about the characteristic deficits of women? Is there any reason why it's a good idea to ascribe to selected groups more or less fixed, even innate, characteristics when it would seem foolish or insensitive or offensive to do the same for other groups? Ought we not to be reluctant—very reluctant—to draw broad conclusions about entire ethnic groups or classes or races? Do we not believe, with the writer Anatole Broyard, that each of us can fashion a singular identity "from [our] own brow," no matter the impediments associated with cultural inheritance or ethnicity?

The sociologist Orlando Patterson has argued, for many years, that no group is definable in terms of fixed characteristics. In fact, he contends, the culture of the United States is "constantly changing" and "open," so that "the accurate metaphor or model" for describing it is "not domination, but dialectic; each group participates and contributes, transforms and is transformed, as much as any other group." What had once seemed "ethnic"—jazz or other forms of black music—"is now part of the wider civilization." Though there was once a reason for blacks especially to think of what was uniquely theirs as a way of defining themselves, Patterson writes, "a continued commitment to ethnicity not only legitimizes the reactionary ethnic revival . . . but more importantly reinforces styles and orientations which are dysfunctional for the group in its attempt to seek an equal place in [the] society." To be sure, Patterson emphasizes, "it was inevitable that [for a long time] the dominant culture [was] actually experienced very painfully," and it was "inevitable, too, that in mobilizing for equality, ethnicity should become an important rallying point [for blacks] since race had been the basis of their exclusion." But a clear-eyed understanding of our common history should cast "any notion of innate ethnicity [as] absolute madness. . . . Traditional ethnic groups," Patterson continues, "are essentially adaptive. By their very nature, they are paving the way for their eventual dissolution," and other kinds of ethnic groups "can opt out of the ethnic mode once [their] political objectives have been achieved." However different from one another, Patterson argues, ethnic groups all betray the fact that to a considerable degree "ethnicity is optional, or chosen," not a fate but the consequence of an exercise of will and imagination.

That view of ethnicity, and of identity itself, is also central to the writing of Edward Said, who was himself deeply invested in the struggles of people in the Arab world to assert their own national identity by rejecting the view of their culture as "congenitally inferior" to Western models "and something of which to be ashamed." Though Said was alert to the problems inherent in the rise, throughout the Arab world, of what were "not only nationalist universities but also political institutions," he regarded this development as an understandable consequence of the "tremendous spiritual wound felt by many of us because of the sustained presence in our midst of domineering foreigners who taught us to respect distant norms and values more than our own."

But then, what was an understandable consequence was also, in a great many ways, a disaster. "All too often in the Arab world," Said writes, "true education was short-circuited," young Arabs "remade in the image of the ruling party," with universities now "the proving ground for earnest patriots," "political conformity rather than intellectual excellence . . . made to serve as a criterion for promotion and appointment with the general result that timidity, a studious lack of imagination . . . came to rule intellectual practice." Where the ethnic revival, under the auspices of the new nationalism, briefly promised at least a robust self-assertion, it came to represent "not freedom but accommodation, not brilliance and daring but caution and fear, not the advancement of knowledge but self-preservation."

Obviously the American university is by no means a reflection of the university in the Arab world. Whatever complaints many of us may wish to make about the wages of identity politics and their effect on American intellectual and academic life, there remains much to admire and protect in the American university. And yet Said's more than cautionary portrait of the Arab university deserves to be taken to heart more than it has been by American academics. When Said writes that the critical intellect "must not be coercively held in thrall to the authority of the national identity," he clearly intends that the words "national identity" be extended to other forms of racial or ethnic identity coercively deployed to keep people in line. To be sure, as he says, there are times when "a long-deferred and -denied identity needs to come out into the open," though that "is only the first step," and "to make all or even most of education subservient to this goal is to limit human horizons."

If the university is a central proving ground for current notions of identity, then what is promoted there, under the auspices of terms like "intersectionality," is bound to affect the larger society in untold and dire ways. Said again: "To assume that the ends of education are best advanced by focusing principally on our own separateness, our own ethnic identity, culture and traditions ironically places us where as subaltern, inferior, or lesser races we had been placed by nineteenth-century racial theory." Again: "The world we live in is made up of numerous identities interacting, sometimes harmoniously, sometimes antithetically. . . . [And thus we cannot] advocate knowledge only of and about ourselves. . . . Inside the academy we should be able to discover and travel among other selves, other identities . . . we should regard knowledge as something for which to risk identity and we should think of academic freedom as an invitation to give up on identity in the hope of understanding and perhaps even assuming more than one."

Extraordinary, that Said should have been willing to propose and to seriously entertain the thought of giving up on identity, at a time when everywhere it seems indispensable, and the determinism it often entails feels somehow not only right but attractive to a great many intelligent people—people who should find tonic and thrilling Said's paean to the traveler who "crosses over, traverses territory, and abandons fixed positions, all the time," in opposition to "the potentate who must guard only one place and defend its frontiers." The investment in ethnicity or gender or transgender or national origin as the single and overmastering truth of an identity has become gospel in several precincts of American society. Oddly, this investment has not entirely done away with an earlier consumerist conception of identity politics, in terms of which people tell themselves that they have freely "chosen" the defining identity they permit to drive and delimit their self-conception.

Here, as elsewhere, attitudes that come across as definite are riddled with confusion. Persons who take their identities—as gay people, as black women, as white males—to be, in effect, obligatory, conferred on them by the gaze of others and the apparent reality of their senses, continue nonetheless to maintain that there is an elective element in their self-definition. The standard line is often of the species "We are what we are and there's no way around that" and yet also "proud to take our stand and to declare a personhood that is essentially one-dimensional." One young woman, an Oberlin College student profiled in a *New Yorker* essay by Nathan Heller, declares that she is "going home, back to the 'hood of Chicago, to be exactly who I was before I came to Oberlin." Another student says she does what she does "because I have *nothing else to do*."

There is nothing in these and other kinds of testimony to reflect Said's sense of the traveler who abandons fixed positions. Another Oberlin student activist who speaks of "other identities—trans folk and all that," and boasts that "we're the generation that's trying to incorporate everybody," is yet fully committed to the language of separate, bounded identities, us and them. To "incorporate everybody" signifies to the student who used that expression, and to a great many other people caught up in the atmosphere generated by identity politics, to make sure that every ethnic or gender or religious entity, conceived as separate tribes with separate agendas, has a place in the society. Said's bracing idea, that we might strive to assume "more than one" identity, is not at all on the horizon of this kind of thinking. The notion that we might want, prefer, to be something of a stranger to ourselves, to see ourselves not as we thought we were but as containing multitudes contending within us in unstable ways, is utterly alien to those who believe they are only what they have been given.

Of course those who are unhappy with anything less than the idolatry nowadays reserved for celebrations of identity will contend that really there is no way out of identity and that it is hopeless to pretend otherwise. Doesn't Said identify himself in terms of "where I originally come from"? Doesn't Orhan Pamuk speak as a Turkish national with certain proclivities he associates with his people and his Turkish generation? Isn't it clear that, even for people who accept that ideas of ethnicity and national identity are never fixed, there cannot be what Charles Taylor calls "a self on one's own," so that there must always be "some reference to a defining community"? I say that I am plural, that I embody what I take to be a multicultural self, and yet I acknowledge that when I speak for myself I rely on the "webs of interlocution" derived from my experience of others who belong, more or less, to the "community of like-minded souls" who are disposed to hear me out and respond. Is this not to lay claim to identity, however tempted we are by the promise of "finding [our] own bearings"?

These are not questions we can hope to resolve. The pastor in Marilynne Robinson's novel *Gilead* likes to say that "in every important way we are such secrets from each other," and everything in Robinson's work would seem to support that assertion. "Every single one of us," the pastor goes on, "is a little civilization built on the ruins of any number of preceding civilizations, but with our own variant notions of what is beautiful and what is acceptable." Our own variant notions. Exactly. Very far, those variant notions, from the identity fixation that would have us speak of our origins as if they owned us, or of race as itself a form of authenticity (or ignominy), or of ethnicity as if it were not at best an opportunity to judge or repudiate what we've been given. "To reduce a nationality . . . to a sectarian political cause is grotesque," writes Ian Buruma. No less might be said for the tendency to reduce race, ethnicity, sexual preference, or gender to the sectarian political cause they have inspired in the era of identity politics.

HOSTILE & UNSAFE:
IDEAS & THE FEAR OF DIVERSITY

. . . that powerful part of modern culture that exists by means of its claim to political innocence and by its false seriousness—the political awareness that is not aware, the social consciousness which hates full consciousness, the moral earnestness which is moral luxury.

—Lionel Trilling

The critic George Scialabba has recently proposed that we must find ways to "lose arguments." After all, he contends, "it's a really efficient way to learn things" and "leads to a very useful habit: not caring who's right." People of my sixties generation supposed that those most likely to censor and despise genuine argument were conservatives, who knew better than to fight about what to them seemed self-evident. But things have changed over the last thirty years, so that David Bromwich can write of the academic Left that, though "they did hope to improve the justice of American society by molding the attitudes of students . . . disagreement with their views was liable, in consequence, to appear censurable as a moral fault," leaving us with "a new strain of intellectual conformity," speech codes and a sense that strenuous argument directed at vital issues is something we might well learn to do without. The robust arguments many of us on the political Left once welcomed and provoked are thus increasingly regarded—by many of our academic colleagues—with hostility and suspicion. Though I find it impossible to imagine a social order I would want to live in that isn't built around an ongoing, even interminable series of arguments, I find that many of my students are decidedly uncomfortable with intellectual combat.

No doubt Yeats was right to warn, a century or so ago, that often in the modern world the best lack all conviction—you know how it goes—while only the worst are full of passionate intensity, so that the arguments, such as they are, will much of the time seem anything but edifying. And yet we do argue, don't we? And we want to be able to continue doing so as if things mattered, and the tools at our disposal were sufficient to allow us to know, more or less, what we're arguing about. A very good friend of mine told me, not long ago, that passionate intensity was overrated, and conviction too, and of course I knew what she meant. People with convictions are much of the time tedious. Moreover, they are intent on achieving a grand consensus and, not incidentally, bringing everyone else to their knees. At best, they want us, the rest of us, to feel free to express ourselves, as they like to say, but only on the condition that we find them and their convictions irresistible and keep our mouths shut when we don't. No surprise, really, that passionate intensity seems often to belong most insistently to the commissars of correctness and their inflamed camp followers, who have as little use for real argument as they have for genuine difference or diversity.

Of course there are arguments and arguments. Reasonable people even find themselves arguing over whether or not there is any special virtue in being reasonable, contending, more than occasionally, and with considerable justification, that reason is only reason and can satisfy only the rational side of our nature. Others—shall we call them postmodernists?—contend that all values are "constructions" and that disputes about ideas are inevitably hopeless and much of the time incoherent, in the sense that people can grasp only what their own culture or tribe or faction allows them to grasp. Meanwhile, legions of the newly enlightened tell themselves that they must strive to eliminate strain and conflict, so that argument itself will seem more and more to be a sign that things are not as they were meant to be, and mere ideas will remind us all of the sorry fact that we have not yet arrived at the one true idea that will banish all the others.

A number of my writer friends say that this is not a good time for ideas. Though people hold them or dismiss them, promote them or disparage them, the ideas are apt often to seem notoriously unstable. Often we think we are debating an idea only to discover that it no longer means what we thought it meant. We proclaim our affection for equality, autonomy, liberation, authenticity only to find that the meanings of these words and the concepts they name have changed utterly into something unrecognizable. Those of us who have long been wary of big ideas, ideas that mobilize infatuates, find that even modest ideas are routinely appropriated for purposes that can only seem astonishing. This is a time, after all, when students and their mentors at major universities declare themselves endangered by the "unsafe and hostile" environment created by a professor—call her Laura Kipnis if you like—who has had the nerve to publish a controversial article. Thought you understood terms like "unsafe," "hostile," and "endangered" and knew more or less what diversity of outlook or opinion might entail in an academic environment? Think again. The very notion of diversity is now increasingly understood to refer to anything but differences of outlook, which we are urged—by the newly enlightened and militant—not to protect but to suppress and eliminate so that no delicate sensibility need be challenged or unsettled. A Jewish proverb says, "Don't wish too hard or you'll get what you want." So, you want to make things safe enough to protect yourself and others not only from shock and awe but from potentially disturbing thoughts and ambivalences? Don't be surprised if you end up with more than you ever bargained for. Mae West liked to say that "too much of a good thing can be a good thing," and who wouldn't say amen to that? But too much *safe* and *secure* and *beneficent* will never add up to anything good.

Of course ideas have always been at least somewhat unstable. The standard, unfavorable sense conveyed by the word "prejudice" was consistently challenged, over centuries, by thinkers like Edmund Burke and, later, T. S. Eliot, who saw in prejudice the goal you hoped to arrive at if you were to have a foundation for your thoughts and any hope of conducting a serious argument. Sartre, in his debates with Albert Camus, made "inviolable values" and "high principles" sound like dirty words. Adam Phillips has stirred many of us to think of "fundamentalism" as a disposition by no means limited to Islamists, extending the concept to anyone for whom certain principles are nonnegotiable and worth dying for.

And yet, in spite of this long history of instability in the domain of ideas, it does now seem compelling to consider that it is harder than ever before to argue about ideas without first ascertaining that you and your antagonist share even rudimentary assumptions about what exactly is intended when a concept is invoked.* Is judgment an exercise of discrimination or, as Montaigne had it, "an expression of habit"? Is "the other" to be understood as external to oneself or as a part of oneself? Is perfectibility to be understood as a delusion or, as Rousseau contended, that which principally "distinguishes us from animals"? When we say "love," are we speaking of "the marriage of true minds" or of Jacques Lacan's idea that "love is giving something you haven't got to someone who doesn't exist"?

Clearly anyone can deplore the evolution or disappearance of particular ideas. Each of us knows how to posture and preen on behalf of ideas that seemed secure and are now regarded as problematic or naive or irrelevant. Whatever happened, we ask, to the idea of color blindness we used to think we aspired to in a multiracial universe and now find too quaint even to mention? Can it be that disinterestedness, once a noble ideal, has become nothing more than the mask that power wears? Is sympathy the good, plain thing we used to call fellow feeling, or has it become one of those coercive fanaticisms wielded by people who never saw a moral high ground they didn't like?

And what ever happened to banality, now that artworks heavily invested in the elementary or the obvious are hung with pride in major museums and bought up at high prices by influential collectors? Can it be that banality no longer signifies anything at all, that the word itself, like the idea it once expressed, has become perfectly

* I was reminded of this quite recently when I sat on a panel with the conservative thinker Patrick J. Deneen, who defines liberalism as "depersonalization and abstraction," the "evisceration of culture," and the systematic elimination of "constraint." No qualification in this caricature. No sense that liberalism is a house with many rooms, or that the caricature in no way describes the liberalism of Martha Nussbaum or Michael Walzer, David Remnick or Jill Lepore. Hard, then, to debate "liberalism" when participants cannot agree on what they are discussing.

meaningless? Not so easy, is it, to note the progress of such an idea without seeming at least to posture and deplore, to wax nostalgic for a time when you could say "banal" with some assurance that others would understand what you were going on about.

To be sure, many ideas that once had much to recommend them deserve in time to disappear. "The sublime," perhaps, or "blaming the victim," or "authenticity" when it refers to characteristics that are thought to be fixed and irrevocable, as in "authentically Jewish" or "authentically black." About such things people can, quite clearly, disagree, and of course I have no program or formula to offer that will settle disputes built around things of this kind, though I can, really I can, smile for days on end when I learn, from a delirious manifesto, that males, authentic males, are "fatally engaged with violence, annihilation, and extinction," all as a result of their obsession with achieving and sustaining erection. So much for "authentic." For ideas that may well deserve, as I say, to disappear.

But the more serious issue has to do with the fact that at present a great many good and vitally important ideas are apt to be misused and are not, as a rule, honorably employed even by persons who should know better. Consider, if only for a moment, the idea of systemic racism. Clearly this is an idea intended to suggest that racism is often embedded in our ways of thinking and feeling even when we are not aware of entertaining anything but beneficent impulses toward persons of color. More, racism is—or may be—reflected in laws and protocols that were not officially designed to prevent or prohibit racial equality but have the effect of accomplishing exactly that. This idea has become so familiar and so widely accepted that it almost seems foolish to challenge it, and in fact even those of us who are astonished at the abuses to which the idea is susceptible are willing to accept that it has helped us to understand a great deal about the persistence of racism in our society. My point here is that even legitimate ideas like systemic racism are often invoked as blunt instruments wielded so as to inhibit real talk and real thinking, along the lines laid out by Kwame Anthony Appiah in an essay published some years ago in the pages of *Salmagundi*, where he speaks of the "racial etiquette" that has made it hard to talk about ideas like systemic racism.

"My impression," Appiah writes, "is that many well-intentioned, non-racist academics . . . who are not black, feel that in criticizing [certain ideas] they risk . . . exposing themselves, dare I suggest, to the risk of being accused" of "contributing to racism." This is not, he goes on, "to put it mildly, in the best interests of learning," and "it is also, often, condescending," reflecting as it does "a refusal to think seriously about racism" and to make it possible to "distinguish racism from other things." And thus do we find that ideas—even ideas like racism, privilege, microaggressions—can come to lead lives unimagined by their progenitors. "Stalking a lost deed," said Milan Kundera forty years ago, of those Czech intellectuals who rapidly found, to their horror, that they had given their allegiance to platinum-plated "progressive" ideas that would soon be used to betray them or silence them.

Of course we have long supposed that so-called liberal societies are worth defending precisely because they are committed to pluralism and the clash of ideas. And yet on several fronts our liberal societies are advancing toward what a number of thinkers call "missionary regimes" promoting what they take to be "advanced values." These values are informed by ideas whose status is—or is felt to be—all but unimpeachable. One such idea is rooted in the belief that if you show people the error embedded in their ways of thinking, you will turn them around and save them from themselves. Explain to the religious that their faith is based on illusion and before you know it their faith will disappear. That sort of thing. Faith itself thus an idea you can refute and displace with a better idea. Nor are advanced thinkers who operate in this way to be found only on the political or cultural Left. In France, to argue for divestment from Israeli enterprises, as a protest against Israeli actions in Gaza, is now regarded not merely as a terrible idea, which perhaps it is, but as a form of incitement to violence and thus a criminal offense. No doubt, in the wake of terrorist attacks in Paris and in other French cities, further restrictions on political discourse will be introduced, always with the standard, high-minded appeals to solidarity and *liberté*. So much for openness and the clash of ideas in a Western enlightenment capital, where the going consensus has it that, if you teach people not to have bad thoughts, you will save them from error, that is, from drawing unwanted conclusions about the things they see, and that you will thereby offer them an ambivalence-free life.

To those who spend much of their time in academic settings, the phenomenon I am associating with missionary regimes will be instantly recognizable. More and more in such settings the learning agenda is controlled by bureaucrats and their academic enablers who, as David Bromwich has described them, regard "learning as a form of social adjustment" and believe that it is their business to promote "adherence to accepted community values."

But then, the life of ideas is also increasingly compromised in precincts beyond the academy. Why should this be so? Clearly it is not sufficient to point to the instability of ideas. In many respects, that is the least of the problems we confront and may not be very much of a problem at all. In fact, the problems to which I've alluded here have principally to do with something else entirely. Call it, if you will, the consequence of a failure, widely shared in our culture, to relate to ideas as if they might be radically incommensurable. Meaning what exactly? Simply, to begin with, that many ideas or values cannot be plausibly or usefully compared. Why not? Because the background presupposed by different ideas, the history and logic informing them, may well be too different for them to be comparable. In accepting incommensurability as between one idea and another, we do not declare that we cannot or will not choose between them, only that neither reason nor logic will certify the correctness of the choice we make. I say that the idea of affirmative action seems to me compelling, though I know it to be a violation of other ideas I honor. Such as? Such as the idea that, in making assessments and commitments, it is essential NOT to assign primary importance to race or gender or ethnicity. The criterion of compensation, or restitution, that informs the idea of affirmative action is essentially distinct from and not comparable with the ideas that inform a principled resistance to affirmative action. There is no coherent political or ethical system that will allow me to assert with confidence the irresistible superiority of affirmative action *as an idea*—much though it seems to me an indispensable component of any commitment to a more just and equitable society. What the journalist Kelefa Sanneh calls the "upbeat language of diversity helps camouflage racial demands that might otherwise seem impolite— or unconstitutional," and even those of us (like myself) who have successfully bought into the logic of diversity, and fully support the imperative of restitution, are often conflicted about what is now required of us when we interview job candidates.

Just so, the idea informing "choice" or "a woman's right to choose" or "abortion rights" is not commensurable with a religiously inspired opposition to abortion, which regards it as a sin to terminate a pregnancy. Proponents of both views, each rooted in fully elaborated ideas, often pretend that the one is clearly superior to the other, when in truth there is no coherent way to compare them. Again, we make our choice, but we deceive ourselves if we suppose that reason is sufficient to validate that choice. It isn't reason that informs Antigone's decision to bury her traitorous brother. In deciding to defy the law, and her uncle the king, Antigone does not compare the one idea of rightful obligation (to the law) with the other (to a brother). Antigone chooses as she must, given who she is. But the essentially incommensurable nature of the ideas at issue cannot be denied or resolved. The tragedy lies in the fact that both conceptions of obligation are legitimate and compelling.

We are not, most of us, tragic characters—I myself try very hard not to be one—and yet we can surely accept that in weighing ideas we will often be dealing with incompatibilities and incomparables, and proceeding without the help of a fully reliable, overarching standard. Liberal societies have, in general, tended to accept what John Gray calls the "agonistic character" of the freedoms we enjoy, and there is a sense in which mundane formulas like "agreeing to disagree" or "respecting difference" presuppose at least a vague appreciation of incommensurability. Not long ago you could quote John Stuart Mill on the "bad and immoral" persons who stigmatize those who hold unpopular opinions, and in quoting him you would know at least that Mill had helped to create

Our educated classes regard the university as an efficient engine for transmitting anxiety about dangerous ideas.

the consensus on which modern liberal societies were built. But that foundation is today not at all secure, and what Mill had to say about English society in 1859, when he published *On Liberty*, seems now extraordinarily pertinent. "In the present age," he wrote, "—which has been described as 'destitute of faith, but terrified at scepticism'—... the claims of an opinion to be protected from public attack are rested not so much on its truth, as on its importance to society." To Mill's observation we might add that, for a great many writers, intellectuals, and academics, the agonistic character of liberal culture no longer seems at all an attractive

How bizarre that a culture officially committed to diversity and openness should be essentially conformist.

proposition. Our educated classes regard the university chiefly as an instrument of our collective purpose and an efficient engine for transmitting anxiety about ideas felt to be dangerous or out of bounds. Bizarre, of course, that a culture officially committed to diversity and openness should be an essentially conformist culture and that the hostility to the clash of incommensurable ideas and even to elementary difference should be promoted with the sort of clear conscience that can only belong to people who don't know what they're doing.

My old friend Irving Howe, who published my first essays in a little magazine called *Dissent* fifty-five years ago, wrote back then that "every current of the zeitgeist ... every assumption of contemporary American life favors the safe and comforting patterns of middlebrow feeling." We don't use expressions like "middlebrow" anymore, but I'd like to suggest that the words "safe and comforting patterns of middlebrow feeling" do accurately identify a good deal of what we contend with. Don't care for "middlebrow" as a handy term of derogation? Bracket it if you like, but also consider that the lockstep march of the new commissars setting up to take control of our cultural institutions, from the universities to the mainstream media, has much to do with creating what Howe called "safe and comforting patterns" of feeling. The favored ideas are informed by—what to call it?—a determination not to offend, not to disorient, not to stir discomfort. The idea of learning as adjustment is rooted in hostility to friction or dispute. What Kwame Anthony Appiah described as conversational etiquette is designed to ensure that conversation remain safe and refuse to stray in the direction of ideas that could conceivably cause anyone to feel fatally set apart from others in one's cohort. The desire to make nice is, so I believe, a staple feature of what Howe calls "middlebrow" feeling.

Inevitably the kind of thing I'm after here will take many different forms, and in proposing analogies or historical antecedents I would never want to suggest that one expression of a political tendency or a cultural formation is equivalent to any other. And yet I have no reluctance at all to invoke at this point a work that meant a great deal to American intellectuals of my generation, not because it addressed "middlebrow" feeling but because it alerted us to a phenomenon oddly renascent in our culture. I'm speaking of Czeslaw Milosz's *The Captive Mind*, a work in which he anatomized the accommodation of Polish intellectuals of the early 1950s to varieties of authoritarianism. Central to Milosz's portraits of typical Polish figures was their desire for what he called "a feeling of belonging," a feeling not always easy to achieve, and thus accomplished, in Milosz's telling, by a ready resort to the "Pill of Murti-Bing," designed to relieve people of doubt and anxiety.

Not surprisingly, many of his contemporaries resisted Milosz's characterization of them, and many of those now teaching in the American academy will likewise resist my efforts to associate what is going on today with the tendency memorably studied by Milosz. They will resist, most especially, the suggestion that they have need of such a pill, and they will deny that they have mastered a way of adapting to the ideological demands of the moment, contending that they have miraculously preserved, as Tony Judt wrote in 2010, "somewhere within themselves the autonomy of a free thinker—or at any rate a thinker who has freely chosen to subordinate himself to the ideas and dictates of others," to persons who pass in this society for the indisputably "enlightened." To be sure, as Judt noted, students and others in the United States will find themselves "mystified" by the notion that anyone would simply capitulate, blithely buy into "*any* idea, much less a repressive one." And yet, in a culture very far removed from early-1950s Poland, the drift of portions of the intelligentsia into the fond embrace of safe and reassuring ideological postures, including an intolerance of ideas and persons felt to be divisive, is an unmistakable feature of the present moment.

In the opening chapter of my 2015 book, *The Fate of Ideas*, I describe my long and difficult friendship with Susan Sontag and note that she was powerfully attracted to the transgressive, to waywardness and incompatibilities, to what another writer called "the instabilities that are the modern condition." Susan was by no means an easy person to be close to, but she was, so I felt, an exemplary intellectual and, for people like me, an odd and improbable authority figure. How so? In her attraction to writers and thinkers who "create themselves," who are "inexorable" in their willingness to think against the grain of received or officially accredited ideas.

When I interviewed her for the first time in 1975—the published version appears as "The 'Salmagundi' Interview" in *A Susan Sontag Reader*—she had just engaged in an extended debate with the poet Adrienne Rich, who had argued that, in criticizing the filmmaker Leni Riefenstahl, Susan had "let down the good [feminist] cause." Sontag's response? "Party lines," she argued, "make for intellectual monotony and bad prose," and result in "demands for intellectual simplicity."

I'm willing to end there, with Sontag, with the sense, embodied in all of Susan's work, that the life of ideas is at best strenuous and incompatible with the rage for "simplicity" and "party lines," and that an educational establishment committed to "accepted community values" will never find a way to honor the transgressive, the inexorable, or the instabilities that are at the heart of "the modern condition."

POLICING DISABILITY

What began as concrete activism *aimed at getting justice devolved* into abstract *gestures* unconcerned with justice.

—John McWhorter

Needless to say, the study of illness and disability has been with us for a long time. Many of us are old enough to recall the excitement generated by Michel Foucault's *Madness and Civilization*, Erving Goffman's *Stigma*, and later works by Susan Sontag (*Illness as Metaphor*) and other writers. These works alerted us to a great many things most of us had never thought to consider. They also made what had seemed obvious suddenly problematic. The British cultural critic Peter Sedgwick noted that "no attribution of sickness to any being can be made without the expectation of some alternative state of affairs which is considered more desirable." That observation, and others like it, opened up an entire field of study that drew attention to the "construction" of illness and the implications inherent in widely shared assumptions about "normality," "deviancy," and the "logic" informing concepts of "human pathology." Over the decades debates have continued to form around one or another dimension of the research and theory generated within this arena. But only recently have particular ideas promoted by academics and health specialists working in disability studies seemed—to some of us, at least—genuinely alarming.

Those particular ideas were lately brought to my attention when I found myself agitated by a poster hung all over campus at the college I've been teaching at for fifty years. A younger colleague had told me about it, and at once I made the rounds, stopping at various department offices to see the thing for myself. A homely thing, in fact, visually no more compelling than most of the notices routinely covering every available surface in hallways and stairwells, the words "KEEP SKIDMORE SAFE" at the head of the new poster not at all unusual at a time when "safety" seems much on many minds.

Of course "safety" can refer to a great many different things, to actual dangers and imagined dangers, to imminent harm and prospective harm, to reasonable and delusional notions of security. There are those for whom the will to safety is so great that the prospect of what Norman Mailer once called "a slow death by conformity with every creative and rebellious instinct stifled" is not at all dreadful. Clearly those who hope to be protected from unfamiliar or challenging ideas demand a kind of safety decidedly different from the safety sought by those who rightly fear violence, sexual abuse, or gross intimidation. Advocates of protections for children with abusive parents are invested in a kind of safety far removed from the safety at issue in campaigns against academic courses that feature primarily dead white males. Whatever the virtues of one or another movement focused on safety, it is essential to think seriously about what can conceivably be gained, or lost, in the event that a consciousness-raising campaign actually succeeds in accomplishing its ends.

The "KEEP SKIDMORE SAFE" poster was, in this respect, a token of drastic changes that have lately come to pass in the academy. Its focus was so-called ableist language, an idea promoted in recent years in numerous courses associated with disability studies. Examples of this ostensibly dangerous species of language, cited on the Skidmore poster, included "stand up for," "turn a blind eye to," and "take a walk in someone's shoes." These expressions are routinely said to be demeaning and offensive by proponents of the campaign targeting such linguistic "abuses." As in other such campaigns, intention is said to be at most an incidental consideration, the "abuse" associated with the willful ignorance or insensitivity of those who use language thoughtlessly. A professor who encourages a student to "take a walk in someone's shoes" may think she is promoting empathy when in fact she is creating an awkward situation for another student who is unable to walk and is thereby painfully reminded of his disability. That, at least, is at the heart of the case not only for strenuously calling attention to ableist language but for doing something about it.

In the early stages of academic disability studies there seemed nothing remotely disturbing about efforts to think about embodiment and normalcy. Why not look closely at the works of gifted writers whose experience of disability allowed them to see the common world in original and sometimes shocking ways? Why not probe language itself so as to reveal the relationship between bodies and metaphor and to expose practices built into ordinary speech? Why not, in fact, move on to ask political questions about the rhetoric of diversity and wonder at the absence of disability issues from the standard conversations built around inclusion? All of that seemed, as I say, not only plausible but valuable, and some of the scholarly research sponsored in the field was rigorous and challenging.

But it is one thing to identify practices and assumptions and another to suppose that they can or should be eliminated. It's one thing to open up a lively conversation and another to promote a conversion narrative in terms of which a cadre of language activists teach everyone else to watch what they say and thereby put an end to practices that are neither injurious nor offensive. Activists in this precinct regard ordinary terms like "blind" and "deaf" as casually denigrating. Such terms are said to reinforce so-called ableist attitudes and thus to foster inequality. More, those kinds of terms are said to be charged with a history of oppression that should alert us to the danger inherent in resorting to such epithets. Though some scholars regard the linguistic emphasis in disability studies as an unfortunate distraction from other kinds of struggle, the focus on language is especially appealing to those with an appetite for calling out and guilt-tripping liberal academics who have not yet gotten with the program.

The "KEEP SKIDMORE SAFE" poster was in this sense a harbinger of things to come in an academic culture increasingly committed to thinking about all things in terms of harms, protections, and legal recourses. Directed at students, drafted (as I was later informed) by Peer Health Educators enrolled in courses taught by health professionals and disability scholars, the message was unmistakable. Specifically, students were encouraged to ask their own teachers to stop using ableist language

We will pay a price for creating a generation unwilling to differentiate between actual offenses and casual utterances.

and, failing that, to contact advisers and file an online "bias report" naming the professor. Informing this message was, of course, an assumption that the mere sounding of words like "blind" and "deaf" ought itself to be regarded as injurious and thus forbidden.

Clearly those responsible for such a message have moved on from any misgiving about their premises and are unwilling to entertain the thought that expressions like those cited in the poster have nothing at all to do with any reasonable person's notion of keeping the campus safe. All apart from the advice that would have students filing a bias complaint, the recommendation that they take offense at the language all of us use is sufficiently bizarre.

Disagreement in this arena will not turn on whether or not it is objectionable to speak respectfully to persons who are disabled. This goes—ought to go—without saying. But the notion that students will feel unsafe when I tell them I have to "run" to catch a train or that I've long been "deaf" to certain kinds of music is a lie. No doubt some students can be trained to take offense where no offense is intended. But there will be a price to pay for creating a generation of young people who are unwilling and unable to differentiate between actual offenses and casual utterances that clearly do not rise even to the level of so-called microaggressions.

A former student assistant, now a close friend, spoke with me about this at a recent dinner party and asked whether I did not sometimes find myself hurt or at least taken aback by a casual ableist affront. I don't think so, I said, though of course at seventy-six and counting I'm old enough to have thought quite a lot about all the things I used to do that are no longer possible for me. But the difference between innocuous speech acts and openly rude or hostile utterances intended to wound, I went on, has always been compelling to me. For example, I offered, I've never quite been able to erase the memory of an encounter in Saul Bellow's novel *Mr. Sammler's Planet* when the elderly protagonist is delivering a lecture and a student in the audience interrupts him with the words, "Why do you listen to this effete old shit? What has he got to tell you? His balls are dry. He's dead. He can't come." If you want to be offended, I told my friend, *there's* something you can sink your teeth into.

And did I think, my young friend asked, that old age is a form of disability? Maybe so, I said, and sure, if I were to sign on to this business and learn to take offense where none was intended, I'd soon discover that just about every conversation had become a minefield, and I'd be accusing even my friends of insensitivity. I'd bristle when a colleague at my dinner table, a Victorian scholar, spoke of Thomas Carlyle's "virile" prose, or of Matthew Arnold's "lame" attempts at humor. Once you start down that road, you rapidly discover that ableist language is not some exotic phenomenon but a pervasive feature of our speech.

In fact, when I read over the poster and decided to write a letter to the professor whose name appeared as the official contact person for "KEEP SKIDMORE SAFE," I first thought to assemble examples of ableist language from Shakespeare, Dickens, and other canonical authors. But then I wondered whether I might instead turn to a contemporary writer whose stature among people in my own left-liberal cohort is especially high, and I thought of Ta-Nehisi Coates, whose book *Between the World and Me* was sent to incoming freshmen the previous year and was a required text in all freshman seminars at the college, including mine. Though I was less than thrilled by the selection of that work, I dutifully discussed it with students in my seminar and found ways to share with them my admiration for Coates's prose. Were there, in Coates's book, examples of ableist language? I hadn't taken note of them when I prepared for my seminar a year earlier, but there the book was, on a crowded shelf in my office, waiting to be scanned. In five minutes of random browsing I found more than a dozen ableist passages, and quoted them in my letter. From page 25: "If the streets shackled my right leg, the schools shackled my left." Same page: "I suffered at the hands of both." From page 33: "The society could say, 'He should have stayed in school,' and then wash its hands of him." And from page 141: "She said this with no love in her eye." And so on.

And the point of this silly exercise? Simply to note that a recent book by one of the most esteemed writers in the country, a book with the imprimatur of our college, is studded with ableist language. In fact, literary prose is more apt than casual or journalistic language to be marked by varieties of metaphor that rely on embodiment. And in composing my letter, which asked that the posters be taken down, I speculated that if Coates were to be recruited to teach at Skidmore, professors who objected strenuously to his language would presumably encourage their students to demand he change his evil ableist ways and, when he refused to conciliate them, urge them to file a bias report naming him as one who had made our campus "unsafe."

It was, in fact, that last piece of advice that made the poster seem to me, and to many of my colleagues, not only problematic but grotesque. I'm willing to agree to disagree with some of my colleagues about the significance of ableist language, but not willing to smile and roll over at the peculiar species of intolerance that is entailed in the idea that users of words like "blind" and "deaf" are guilty of actionable offenses. The professor to whom I sent my letter responded in an entirely thoughtful and courteous way, noting that she hadn't officially approved the poster designed by students she was working with and that she shared my "concerns" and was therefore moving to have the posters removed. This seemed to me a welcome conclusion to what was, after all, a very tiny affair.

And yet I don't want quite to leave it at that, not when department heads and other faculty at colleges and universities are more or less on board with efforts to enlist students in their misguided campaigns. Underwriting these efforts is the wish to create a hierarchy of the saved—those, for example, who mobilize to forbid routine speech acts weirdly deemed offensive—and the unredeemed: those who persist in any practice of which the new guardians disapprove.

Colleagues ... invested in the moral one-upmanship, in terms of which a self-anointed elect dictate to everyone else what is and is not acceptable.

Colleagues sympathetic to these recent campaigns, however ill at ease about what they call the "too-quick turn to punitive measures," as one colleague put it to me in an email communication, are nevertheless unapologetically invested in the moral one-upmanship, in terms of which a self-anointed elect dictate to everyone else what is and is not acceptable.

Odd, of course, that people determined to extinguish hostility and intimidation are themselves open to a regime in which disapproval leads more or less inexorably to censure and punitive measures. If anything like the "KEEP SKIDMORE SAFE" poster were to be taken seriously—as seriously as numbers of students told me it is among their classmates—and acted on, it would cause members of the college community to become suspicious of one another, to sniff around for instances of language crimes, and to search for opportunities to ingratiate themselves with the local thought police. It's hard to imagine a better example of a hostile work environment, and no optimism about what one colleague calls "a new awareness of inequities" and a desire to "spread the word" can cover over the alarming features of the zealotry unleashed in movements of this kind.

To be sure, the usual persuasion for which campuses have lately mobilized tends to be friendly rather than openly punitive. But the informing consensus is that in due course everyone will be on board and that the recalcitrant will be dealt with, one way or another. Though students especially are convinced that they are coming of age and learning to think for themselves, they have no misgiving at all about yielding to guardians who promise to protect them from unwanted ideas or utterances. Though they bristle at the thought of domination, they don't at all object to domination by the right-minded, and those who have learned to mouth the platitudes served up in their consciousness-raising classes have no sense that they are "brilliant," as Scott Fitzgerald once put it, "with 2nd hand sophistication." But then, neither do the professors themselves often note their own lack of what Rochelle Gurstein calls "the conceptual resources" to think about "the common good," paralyzed as they are by "habits of mind [that allow] them to mistake their ever more sentimental valorization of the most 'vulnerable' in society for a commitment to radical politics."

In effect, our institutions of higher learning have fostered a new paternalism, promising an environment in which surveillance is the norm and citizens need not worry that they have been delivered into the hands of persons whose sole reason for being is to protect them from discomfort. Most of those who have signed on for this arrangement have come to believe that there is self-fulfillment in tacitly resigning themselves to a species of carefully structured subordination. But what one writer calls "dependence as a way of life" entails the gradual erosion of the conviction that we can, all of us, find ways to cope with things that belong to the fabric of everyday experience. No one doubts that there is a place, and a need, for the helping ministrations of family, friends, teachers, and health-care professionals. But we ought not to doubt that we should feel equipped to contend with ordinary unhappiness and the small shocks and contradictions we are bound to confront. The idealization of autonomy and self-sufficiency was always somewhat misleading. But the turn to the idea of a fully administered, indisputably correct, and ever-watchful regime, academic or otherwise, in which miscreants can be admonished and punished for inviting someone to walk in another person's shoes, is the leading edge of a new—and by no means benevolent—tyranny.

HIGH ANXIETY:
THE ATTACK ON *APPROPRIATION*

The image of traveler depends not on power but on motion, on a
willingness to go into different worlds, use different idioms, and
understand a variety of disguises, masks, and rhetorics.

—Edward Said

So: Aren't you sort of annoyed when you read something and you
can tell right away that the writer has appropriated what belongs
to someone else and hasn't even apologized or asked anybody's
permission? That was the question put to Jamaica Kincaid one
July afternoon at the New York State Summer Writers Institute
by an intrepid graduate student. Surprising, Jamaica said, that
you think I'd be annoyed. I mean, I've heard the complaint about
appropriation before, she went on, and I just don't understand
what it's about. It's a complaint, you know, that's bound to come
from people who don't know what goes into making something
like a novel or a painting.

A version of the same question was put, by graduate and under-
graduate students, to other writers throughout the July program—to
Allan Gurganus, Francine Prose, Caryl Phillips, Joyce Carol Oates,
Darryl Pinckney, Russell Banks, and others—and each time the
response was a version of Jamaica's courteous but disillusioning
refusal to concede anything to a notion that had attracted a large

following. An elementary idea had somehow become an *idée fixe*, and I soon saw that it would take more than the testimony of mere writers and artists to dislodge it.

The case against appropriation is rooted in several assumptions. One is that the cultural forms, experiences, and history of a people are a property they can rightly own, and that the owners are thus rightly obliged to defend what is theirs against the predations of others. Recent eruptions—focused on a high-profile Taiwanese athlete wearing dreadlocks or a black athlete sporting Chinese tattoos on his biceps or an American rock star (Rihanna) attending a Costume Institute affair in an "imperial yellow" gown designed by a Chinese couturier—suggest that those who are invested in this issue have no wish to differentiate between predation and homage, and that the notion of ownership can extend from hairstyles to footwear, from mundane artifacts to poetic iconography. Though it would seem obvious to say that these kinds of objections are often misguided and that no group can own an image or a trope or a fashion, the will to register insult and to complain of violation is so pronounced in so many quarters of the culture that the obvious will no longer seem so.

A further assumption underwriting the case against appropriation is that it simply isn't possible for artists without the lived experience of the situation or condition they wish to capture to adequately represent it. This is felt to be especially true when the experience at issue belongs to marginalized people, and even the supposedly good intentions of artists from "privileged" backgrounds—white persons—cannot prevent them from doing damage, promoting stereotypes, spreading falsehood. Francine Prose notes that already we can see the results of this increasingly widespread assumption, where "books are being categorized—and judged—less on their literary merits than on the identity of their authors." More, the absurdity entailed in this way of thinking about books and artists is not at all registered by those in thrall to these assumptions. Consider, Prose asks, "how can one write a historical novel if one has no 'lived experience' of that period?" Must we not "dismiss *Madame Bovary* because Flaubert lacked 'lived experience' of what it meant to be a restless provincial housewife?" Though proponents of "lived experience" are notoriously reluctant to follow out the logic informing their convictions, they might at least concede that in effect they are prepared to censure much of the art and literature that most of us admire—not merely canonical works but the contemporary efforts of many of our best writers.

Nor is this way of anathematizing and dismissing artworks limited to academics and journalists who have swallowed the Kool-Aid. What Prose refers to as "the popular Twitter hashtag #ownvoices" routinely, on principle, "steers readers away from books that feature marginalized characters that have been written by 'authors who aren't part of that marginalized group,'" so that artists and writers who do what the most ambitious and gifted writers and artists have always done are now pilloried by legions of inflamed defenders of the new faith. Online sites are of course notable for the virulence of the attacks unleashed, and the "lived experience" standard has predictably been invoked by throngs of would-be cultural guardians who have already had some success in scaring artists and writers away from subjects that do not clearly belong to them. But more worrying by far is the related effect of this campaign, in that "writers from every group," as Prose argues, are thus discouraged "from describing the world as it is, rather than the world we would like."

Of course the case against appropriation might well have assumed an entirely different form. It might have been focused on genuine issues and genuinely offensive instances and would thus at least resemble a serious critical enterprise. Criticism at its best does, after all, tend to hold books and artworks accountable for actual violations of plausibility, fairness, even propriety. Critics have always routinely asked whether or not a particular work is adequate to the task it sets itself. When Zadie Smith looks at a painting called *Open Casket* by an artist named Dana Schutz, she doesn't complain that a white woman has had the temerity to deal with a subject that can be fairly represented only by a black person. But she does reasonably ask whether the work conveys the weight and emotional intensity of the event it purports to represent. That is, in every respect, a legitimate question to ask, and it does have something at least to do with the issue of appropriation, in that the Schutz painting does clearly allude to an iconic photograph of Emmett Till, murdered in a 1955 incident that continues to stir the imagination of Americans still troubled by race matters and drawn to the history of an enduring conflict. Whatever the formal achievement of the Schutz painting, it was necessary, in dealing with it, for Smith to consider its adequacy and its relation to the iconic photograph it alludes to. To find the Schutz painting deficient, as Smith does, is not to build a case against appropriation but to argue that this particular painting fails to accomplish what it might have done or purported to do.

Just so, it has always been necessary to ask whether particular artworks do plausible justice to their subjects, and to ask about the peculiar relationship between a source and its later incarnation in a parallel work. This ought to go without saying. Why wouldn't a critic ask what J. M. Coetzee has made of the material he "appropriated" from Defoe's *Robinson Crusoe* when he wrote the novel *Foe*? Of course we are interested in the virtues and defects of the particular "appropriation" involved in Jean Rhys's novel *Wide Sargasso Sea*, given its relation to Charlotte Brontë's *Jane Eyre*. What reader of Caryl Phillips's novels would not wish to ask questions about his inspired and challenging "appropriation" of material from *Othello* or *Wuthering Heights* or the life of Anne Frank?

Unfortunately, the concern with appropriation, however legitimate when pursued by readers and critics actually invested in raising important questions, is more often pursued by people who know, even before they have asked the essential questions, what they hope to find. In a recent class on political fiction one of my own students— an especially gifted and articulate young woman—strenuously objected not only to the text we were discussing (Nadine Gordimer's novel *The Pickup*) but to our way of dealing with sensitive material in the novel. The complaint against my selection of the novel was that its author was a white woman attempting to deal with a black man whose experience—of race, of poverty and religion—she could not possibly represent. This complaint the student voiced at a moment in our class discussion when she could "no longer tolerate where this thing is headed," provoked by a question I had raised about the Islamic environment of the African community to which the black husband in the novel had brought his new wife. "What," my student asked, "did you expect a student to say when asked such a question? Of course you want us to say that the white woman is surprised by what she sees, and of course this is all designed to reveal that these supposedly primitive people are bound to be disappointing to someone from a Western society. Here you can see why it's always a bad idea for a white writer to be sticking her nose into this kind of thing, and why assigning these kinds of books to students can only confirm the cultural bias you yourself can't help sharing with the white author you so much admire."

It's not often that one of my students will complain about my selection of course texts or, indeed, about my "designs" or intentions, and given that the assigned readings for that particular course included works by Chinua Achebe, Michael Ondaatje, Anita Desai, and Orhan Pamuk, among others, it had never occurred to me that my choices might be vulnerable to complaint. But my student—as I was soon to learn in a lengthy conversation we later enjoyed in my office—had been through two other courses in which appropriation had been front and center, and she was primed to be offended by what she took to be the intentions informing the novel and, by extension, my own goals in teaching it. Though I spent a good deal of time assuring the student that Gordimer's work, much of it focused on race and race relations, had seemed impressive not only to white men like me but to Nelson Mandela, Bishop Desmond Tutu, and a wide range of writers, black and white, she insisted that it was "nevertheless a bad idea" for a "privileged" white woman to be dealing with people about whose lives "she was bound to be clueless."

And were there particular instances in the novel, I asked her, where Gordimer seemed to her "clueless" and had clearly gotten things wrong? She couldn't say. And was it her sense that the students in the class who responded to her outburst—before I myself jumped in—were mistaken when they pointed out that the white wife at the center of the novel not only registers accurately what is unfamiliar to her in the Islamic environment she enters but soon decides that she feels better about herself as a human being in that environment and eventually refuses to leave it, even when her husband flies off to find employment in the West? "No, of course I saw that," my student conceded, "and yet I didn't like the way the questions you were asking were designed to get students to say how bad things were in that place, how weird it was that the wives couldn't sit and eat until the men were finished, and how backward the attitudes were in general. I mean," she went on, "that it all felt very anti-Islamic, and that Gordimer had appropriated this material, which didn't belong to her, in ways that just confirmed the usual Western prejudices." But wasn't it clear that Gordimer did not confirm those prejudices, I asked, and that we were reading her novel as a prime example of the effort to break through those prejudices? "I can only repeat," my student answered, "that I felt very uncomfortable about the direction we were heading in."

Of course a single instance proves nothing at all, and I myself had to feel that the particular student, who went on to enroll in another course with me the following semester, was to be commended for her forthrightness and courage, though also I felt that she had learned all too well the lessons taught to her in those earlier courses on appropriation. Would she try at least to rethink what we had debated? She would, though my sense was that she had invested too much in the pieties and assumptions she embraced to let go of them.

Like other ideas that have acquired an aura of sophistication, "appropriation" is often invoked as a strategy to ward off unpleasant thoughts—the kinds of thoughts sparked by the works of writers like Gordimer, or, for that matter, other novels included on my course syllabus. Consider, just for a moment, Orhan Pamuk's memoir *Istanbul*, a great and beautiful book that many tell me they find disturbing and uncomfortable. Why uncomfortable? Because Pamuk is notoriously susceptible to second thoughts about his own sentiments and deftly stirs agitation and ambivalence in readers. When he is dealing with appropriation—one among many ideas he handles in his book—he does so not to confirm a prejudice or to curry favor with a reader like my young student but to uncover what is genuinely confounding in what are often complex transactions. To be sure, Pamuk does note, at several points, instances of the very cultural biases that inform legitimate complaints about certain kinds of appropriation. André Gide, Pamuk says, was one of many writers who came to Turkey a hundred years ago and "boast[ed] that his travels have taught him that western civilization . . . is superior to all others." At the same time, Pamuk goes on, Turkish writers at the time, "in their heart of hearts . . . feared Gide's insults might be well-founded," and soon after Gide's work was published, "Atatürk, the greatest westernizer of them all, instituted a revolution in dress, banning all clothing that wasn't western." Uncomfortable? To be sure. Disturbing? By all means, and of course we want and expect no less from a writer who regards everything with a blend of misgiving and bemusement.

Obviously there is much more to say about Gide's appropriations—for example, his depiction of sexually available adolescent boys in the North African setting of a novel like *The Immoralist*—but for Pamuk the insights he is after belong not to a grievance or to the settling of scores but to an interrogation that will often prove unsettling. Unsettling in what sense? In effect, Pamuk works at that question over the entire course of his memoir, where he anatomizes the experience of a culture—his own Turkish culture—perpetually living out its deepest conflicts under Western eyes, alert to its own history of decline and fall, savoring its peculiar blend of pathos and the species of "sweet melancholy" conjured by the term *hüzün*. Pamuk labors mightily to convey the precise flavor and significance of *hüzün*, much in the way that Milan Kundera (in *The Book of Laughter and Forgetting*) labored to convey the meaning of the "untranslatable" word *litost*, and as Gregor von Rezzori (in *Memoirs of an Anti-Semite*) did with the word *skushno*. Each of these writers acknowledges that translation itself is a kind of appropriation and that its objective is bound always to remain at least somewhat out of reach. In Pamuk, one mark of the failure to successfully capture *hüzün* is cited in Claude Lévi-Strauss's efforts to associate it with "tristesse," an approximation by no means adequate: "The *tristesse* that Lévi-Strauss describes," Pamuk writes, "is what a Westerner might feel as he surveys those vast poverty-stricken cities of the tropics, as he contemplates the huddled masses and their wretched lives. But he does not see the cities through their eyes. *Tristesse* implies a guilt-ridden Westerner who seeks to assuage his pain by refusing to let cliché and prejudice color his impressions. *Hüzün*, on the other hand, is not a feeling that belongs to the outside observer. To varying degrees, classical Ottoman music, Turkish popular music, especially the *arabesque* that became popular during the 1980s, are all expressions of this emotion, which we feel as something between physical pain and grief."

Pamuk differentiates *hüzün* from *tristesse* not to indict Western writers for a failure of sympathy in their efforts to understand a peculiarly Turkish sentiment, and not, certainly, to argue that such efforts are inevitably misguided or worse. But he does wish to suggest that within each culture there is a core of feeling that an outside observer will have a hard time understanding. As a result, efforts to appropriate and fairly represent what is elusive may well seem inadequate, even where intentions are good, and the outside observer has made strenuous efforts to allow for discrepant modes of feeling. Only a fool would wish to forbid efforts to reach across those divides or to represent what may well seem obscure. And even within one's own culture, Pamuk argues, there are bound to be, much of the time, varieties of incomprehension and division. *Hüzün* can seem to one who lives within its soft, unremitting embrace either "resignation . . . the outcome of life's worries and great losses" or, to another inhabitant, "their principal cause." For some residents of Istanbul, Pamuk argues, "*hüzün* does not just paralyze the inhabitants [of the city]; it also gives them poetic license to be paralyzed." For other inhabitants, "the honor we derive from it can be misleading."

Try, with these irresolvable contradictions, to insist on a single correct way to translate or appropriate the precise core of feeling entailed in the recourse to *hüzün*, and inevitably you find yourself willing what cannot be willed. And consider as well that the distinguished Franco-Turkish writer Elif Shafak has written: "I do not think *hüzün* is the word that embodies the gist of Istanbul, as Pamuk claims. Istanbul is a vibrant city that throbs, grows and pulsates with endless energy and hunger. . . . And my generation in Turkey is not a generation of melancholy."

And thus it is that, where essential matters are concerned, even writers within a given culture may differ—a fact that would seem obvious were it not for the exertions of many ostensibly sensitive persons, who would have us believe that they are in possession of the indisputable truth about their culture and about what ought to be forbidden to outsiders, who are said to transgress merely by virtue of their efforts to reach across the divide that separates them from others. Appropriation, then, more often than not, is a fraught encounter, though again, the increasingly popular notion that such encounters are hopelessly predatory is not at all what writers like Pamuk and Shafak would have us believe.

In recent decades the cultural relationship between the West and other regions, between so-called Orient and Occident, has frequently been associated with the term "orientalism," a "point of departure," according to Edward Said, for studies of "the right of formerly un- or mis-represented human groups to speak for and represent themselves." These groups, Said contends, "were supposed ... to be confined to the fixed status of an object frozen once and for all in time by the gaze of western percipients." Where "Europe's interlocutor" was wanted, Said argues, the standard scholarship associated with orientalism imposed on its frozen object a "muteness," the status of "its silent Other." The work of recent decades has thus been to dispute the "authority and objectivity" of orientalist scholarship and to find ways to permit all of the "un- or mis-represented human groups"—by no means limited to persons from the "region of the world called the Orient"—to speak for themselves.

The case against orientalism is by now familiar, and though Said and others who prosecuted the case have been subjected to sometimes harsh, sometimes persuasive criticism, the virtues of their case remain obvious. Also obvious is the fact that Said and his cohort never intended the case they made to suggest a categorical opposition to appropriation. Quite the contrary. Said often spoke in praise of efforts to represent the other, and occasionally in praise of ideological opponents whose imaginative sympathy he admired. But Said—as noted by Christopher Hitchens and others—became increasingly "alarmed by the effect he was having in the academy" in the decades following the publication of his famous book *Orientalism*. In an essay on "The Politics of Knowledge" he recounts hostile interactions with academics at a public lecture who upbraid him for failing, for example, to mention "living non-European non-males, even when it was not obvious to me ... what their pertinence might have been." Categorical demands thus were invoked in "place of evidence, argument, discussion." Said's impression, here and elsewhere, was that his own work on orientalism had somehow generated "flat-minded examples of thinking . . . so rigidly constricted" as to persuade only "an audience of like-minded, already fully convinced persons."

There is little question that, had Said lived to see the marketing of standards associated with gender or ethnicity or race to evaluate and proscribe works of art, he would surely have objected to what Hitchens calls the "bleak occasions of dogmatism in the academy." Said, after all, was a lover of what he himself called "intransigence, difficulty, and unresolved contradiction" in works of art, and he refused—in essays like "Orientalism Reconsidered"—to subscribe to any fixed notion of a "real, true, or authentic" identity ("as if Islam were one simple thing") that would forbid imaginative access to others.

In fact, the demand that persons formerly denied a voice be allowed and encouraged to speak has opened up further prospects for appropriation. One of the most powerful and affecting of recent novels is *The Meursault Investigation* by the Algerian journalist Kamel Daoud. The novel is spoken in the voice of Harun, who tells the story of his brother Musa, the anonymous Arab casually murdered by Meursault in Albert Camus's novel *The Stranger*. The essential purpose of the narrative is announced in the opening pages of Daoud's work, where Harun tells us that he means to "speak in the place of a dead man, so I can finish his sentences for him," "take the stones from the old houses the colonists left behind, remove them one by one, and build my own house, my own language." He concedes that "your hero" (Meursault) wrote "so well that his words are like precious stones" and was "a man very strict about shades of meaning," able to make even murder "sound like poetry." The problem, of course, so far as Harun is concerned, is that "The only shadow is cast by 'the Arabs,' blurred, incongruous objects left over from 'days gone by,' like ghosts, with no language except the sound of a flute," the brother Musa at best "a brief Arab, technically ephemeral, who lived for two hours and has died incessantly for seventy years, long after his funeral . . . killed by a bullet fired by a Frenchman who just didn't know what to do with his day," and has thus inspired in Harun, whenever he goes over the story "in my head," a combination of anger and determination.

Though there is much more to say about the novel, and the revenge plot it sets in motion, for our purposes it seems important only to note that the novel is itself an act of appropriation, what one reviewer called a "tour-de-force reimagining of Camus's [novel], from the point of view of the mute Arab victims." But it might also be noted that the novel functions simultaneously as homage (to Camus and his novel) and rebuke, and that its complex handling of material led, in parts of the Arab world, to "demands for [Daoud's] public execution." Of course those demands were not focused on the crime of appropriation but on passages in which Harun shares his instinct for "impieties" and "sacrilege," his detestation of "religious fanatics," his conviction that "God is a question, not an answer." And though one thing is not identical to another, and analogies are always somewhat dubious, it might yet be noted that, in the United States, at the present moment, where no one is calling for the public execution of writers, there are certainly fanatics incensed by what they take to be the unpardonable crime of appropriation, and thus demanding, for example, in a public letter signed by dozens of artists, that the painting *Open Casket* by Dana Schutz be not only taken down from the walls of the Whitney Museum but "destroyed."

And is there, in all of this attention lately paid to appropriation, the prospect of a protest—by inflamed Western partisans of correctness—against the sort of thing represented by Daoud's novel? Apparently Daoud is safe, more or less, by virtue of the simple fact that he is nonwhite and non-Western, and thus by definition permitted to make works of art as he pleases. Of course our homegrown fanatics will be unhappy about the fact that he goes out of his way, in the novel, to praise the writing of Camus, and that he opens with an epigraph from the haute European writer Emil Cioran, and entertains the possibility that, for his sins in depicting his own culture, he may well be "stoned to death." Unpleasant, unsavory, unwanted, these reminders that Daoud really is a free man and, for all his determination to give a voice to one who had been silent, a writer who has appropriated, for purposes by no means so simple and unitary as the "flat-minded" among us would wish.

The idea that only nonwhite artists should be able to appropriate with impunity is one of those generous ideas promoted by persons who believe that in principle we owe to those who have been marginalized in the past a special dispensation, allowing them to take liberties that should properly be forbidden to others. And yet in practice even sponsors of this idea often find themselves unhappy with the results of their sponsorship. For the most part, of course, they have little interest in the predations of white artists who appropriate the works of other white artists. The Anglo-Irish novelist John Banville is thus free to base an entire novel called *Mrs. Osmond* on Henry James's *The Portrait of a Lady*, Picasso well within his rights to make paintings deriving from Velázquez or Poussin or Cranach or Delacroix. No one objects to Anthony Hecht's "Dover Bitch" as an impertinent theft of material stolen from Matthew Arnold's "Dover Beach." But a great contemporary black artist like Kara Walker has been sharply taken to task by other black artists for the use she has made of her models and borrowings. Darryl Pinckney notes that Walker was early condemned "by some black artists . . . for using what they considered stereotypical black images from the nineteenth century that they claimed spoke primarily to a white audience." Others have noted that Walker's work is too invested in images that belong to a received history, particularly a history evoked in popular engravings and photographs. Walker herself openly notes that she has drawn not only inspiration but pictorial structures from artists like Thomas Eakins, Delacroix, and Jean-Léon Gérôme. Alert as she is to the plain fact that the objections to this aspect of her work reflect a radical failure of understanding, and determined to go her own way, Walker mockingly acknowledges the conditions obtaining in the contemporary art scene in the press release for a recent exhibition of her work at Sikkema Jenkins gallery in Chelsea, which includes the following: "Students of Color will eye her work suspiciously and exercise their free right to Culturally Annihilate her on social media."

Pinckney is not alone in noting that often the titles of Walker's paintings, constructions, and silhouettes "set the mood . . . set you up," in ways that ought to somewhat assist viewers who are ill at ease with what she makes of her appropriations and provocations. But more important is his observation that "the texts of her catalogs can be intimidating in their pretended didacticism," and that the images themselves—even those apparently straightforward in their retributive fury—are characteristically disorienting. The inscribed "racial history has broken free and is running amuck," Pinckney writes, the brutal, ugly, and deformed in her work oddly elegant, even beautiful, the black figures often drawn "from different eras and circumstances of black representation," not to mention other sources, "from Disney's *Jungle Book* film" to a "Jazz Age fashion magazine." To speak of appropriation in Kara Walker is to confront a dizzying array of moves, underwritten by a sovereign artist who, for all of her commitment to a racially charged aesthetic, is by no means an ideologue operating from a simple program. No one who has spent hours with her work can be at all surprised to learn that she was one of several prominent black artists who defended Dana Schutz when others demanded that her painting at the Whitney be taken down and destroyed.

But think again of the words "pretended didacticism" and what they conceivably suggest about Walker's paintings themselves. "Didacticism" is not at all a word that first comes to mind when we look at Walker's works, though in some of them there is a literalism, an explicit invocation of brutalities visited on black people that may well inspire a viewer to suppose that the works are calls to take arms, revolt, and rage. Look at *Scraps*, Pinckney proposes, an ink-and-collage work depicting "a naked young black girl in a bonnet, with a small ax raised in her left hand . . . making off with the large head of a white man. She might even be skipping." Is this image an invitation to violence? A celebration? A didactic lesson in what is coming or ought to come? Pinckney notes that "This isn't Judith; it's a demented Topsy in her festival of gore." The terms of choice here—"demented," "festival of gore," "Topsy" (a figure out of Harriet Beecher Stowe)—all suggest a histrionic, performative instigation. Retributive violence is an idea we are forced to entertain, perhaps to embrace, the didactic element central to Walker's work the raising of a question (What if? Why not?) we dare not answer.

Appropriation, clearly, is but one of several options for thinking about what you have when a black person—Walker is one such—is moved to take what she wants and use what she will.

In the face of such work, the attempt to think about appropriation as a clear-cut transaction in which one finished, delimited, boundaried work by an individual is "stolen" and thereby diminished by the related exertions of another is to misconceive entirely what is at issue. The attack on appropriation is premised on a false idea of art making and artworks, on the idea that in the end an art object is a final solution to a problem, a way of excluding other solutions and warding off the efforts of competitors. Tempting, to be sure, the notion that a novel or a painting may rightly be regarded as an entity with a definite set of purposes and directives (violence now?) that an ostensibly alien spirit can only betray—especially when the alien spirit is that of an ethnic or racial "other."

But then, proponents of this way of regarding cultural "properties" and transactions would do well to consider—in the domain of art—how very unreliable is the standard notion of coherent, unambiguous messages and entities. Even casual references to "American identity" or "black identity" are bound to be misleading, all apart from their irrelevance in assigning value to particular works of art. Monolithic conceptions of whiteness or blackness, like grotesque racialist stereotypes purporting to differentiate one set of inherent characteristics from others, are of no use in thinking about what matters in a first-rate painting or novel. The notion that works of art are created to promote "ideas" that can only be jealously defended by an ethnic group that identifies absolutely with those ideas is flatly contradicted by the works themselves—when they are worth anything at all. After all, the spirit governing a complex work will often have much to do with irony and pretense and irresolution.

Ask what exactly is involved in an appropriation, when the object of your inquiry is clearly more ambiguous than you had imagined, and the prospect of lodging a simpleminded objection is apt to seem more dubious than you would perhaps have supposed.

Andrew Delbanco, among others, has sought to remind us that "writers present have always felt the parental presence of writers past," citing "large acts of homage" in the work of Ralph Ellison, Philip Roth, and other American writers. "To read, say, Gish Jen's novel *Typical American*," Delbanco goes on, "or Chang-rae Lee's *Native Speaker* . . . is to be struck by how a few changes in the scenic incidentals, or a few substitutions of Yiddish for Chinese or Korean phrases, would render these works, with their historically recurrent tale of Old World parents versus New World children, almost indistinguishable in plot and structure from [numbers of] Jewish immigrant novels." The goal of such observations is not to challenge the force or originality of the works cited but to indicate that the life of culture is sustained and promoted by people who have a stake in it and "aspire to become part of it," not by people who want mainly to draw lines in the sand and forbid the free play of the imagination. Of course we know that really nothing is entirely "free," that we are all constrained by systems and by the histories we inherit, like it or not. But then, we can manage, surely, to express our skepticism about claims to freedom and transcendence without pretending that there is no difference between artistic freedom and the regime sought by those who

The problem with appropriation anxiety is that it betrays an unwarranted fear of contamination.

would deny to artists the possibility of borrowing and adapting what they will.

In an odd way the attack on appropriation calls to mind the sober exertions of persons in the past who were anxious about the dangers of modernity and intent on setting up an inquisitorial cultural regime to guard against the taking of liberties felt to endanger us all. What Henry James described as "the old Puritan moral sense, the consciousness of sin and hell," is strangely emergent once more in the prescriptive urgencies of stern, would-be cultural guardians who dispense authoritative-sounding directives about what is and is not permitted to artists and, by extension, to the rest of us who would study them, teach them, and celebrate them. "It was a necessary condition," James wrote, "for a man of [Nathaniel] Hawthorne's stock that . . . his imagination should take license to amuse itself . . . to take liberties and play tricks" and to engage even grave matters "from the poetic and aesthetic point of view, the point of view of entertainment and irony." This license, and the sinister, mischievous "irony" that informs Kara Walker's "pretended didacticism," are now suspect, increasingly susceptible to attack by those who would deny to such artists their ambivalence and, it may be, their recourse to the source works they have studied and absorbed.

The problem with appropriation anxiety is that it betrays an unwarranted fear of contamination. "Purity," writes Ian Buruma, "is often the compulsive aim of those who feel they have to make up for their complexity" and are "defensive about their identity." The attack on appropriation is typically launched by people who fear that the single salient virtue of a work (or an experience)—the simple fact that it "belongs" to a "marginalized" group or individual—ought not to be compromised or taken over by anyone else. Buruma is not alone in associating this instinct with narcissism. Leon Wieseltier described it as "the idolatry of origins." The angry expression of appropriation anxiety, on the part of Western academics especially, allows for what Buruma calls a "feeling of vicarious virtue," in terms of which they can identify with those whose "signifying and representing functions," as Said writes, have been usurped. The problem, alas, is that there is no actual virtue in the expression of this anxiety, premised as it is on a series of falsehoods about art and about identity itself.

In the face of recent eruptions, some writers have tried to find what seems to them a middle way to deal with the so-called problem of appropriation. What is a middle way? Claudia Rankine* suggests that we would do well not to leap to "prohibition" when we debate the issue. Better, by far, for those who appropriate to ask themselves whether their imaginative sympathies "line up" with "the lines drawn by power." If so, then they must do better, not necessarily by attempting to speak "from the point of view of characters of color" but by seeking to "expose" the "dynamic" that allows artists to make art without expressly acknowledging the conditions that govern our lives. The demand here is for artists to move beyond assuming their right to make what they will, and to challenge or "undermine" their "own sense of authority." This, Rankine argues, will not be easy; in fact, for writers to challenge their "own sense of authority" is to learn to proceed without "innocence," that is, to accept that, even if they "meant well," their appropriation of the experience of others may be radically deficient, even "irresponsible."

---

* The quotations from Claudia Rankine are taken from the preface to *The Racial Imaginary*, edited by Rankine and Beth Loffreda.

In several respects this seems to me an admirable though by no means successful effort to get past the problem—insofar as it is, in fact, at all reasonable to regard it as a problem. The determination to banish "innocence" and to try to be skeptical about one's own "authority" is reasonable, though the authority exercised by an artist addressing her own work is by no means the danger to others Rankine would have us believe it is. No doubt, as she says, the language of "rights" is unsuitable for the discussion of the creative imagination, though she is not especially persuasive when she asks, "Who can't hear the aggression in 'I have a right of access to whomever I wish'?" Do writers we respect issue declarations so utterly without nuance or misgiving? I hear no aggression in the characteristic declarations of sovereignty issued by writers, and see no unspeakable aggression in the works of artists—of Anselm Kiefer or Gerhard Richter, Hannah Höch or Kerry James Marshall—who freely and unapologetically take what they need. Rankine asks that a writer "be in skeptical tension with her own inclinations," and of course that skepticism is everywhere apparent in the works of ambitious artists.

Again, and try as I may, I don't at all see that Rankine's scruples have rightly to do with appropriation, much though she repeats, insistently, that she is making a case against those who say that it is "against the nature of art itself to place limits on who or what I can imagine." Would a writer of Rankine's sophistication want to declare the contrary, namely, that artists *should* in fact place limits on what they can imagine? Would she have artists subordinate their own imagination to the dictates of a committee for public safety, a creative writing department, a battalion of censors? Why should a writer not think herself free to imagine what it's like to be someone entirely different from her? Why should she not consider that, in imagining what she's not imagined before, she might well discover bracing and important things, about herself and others? Why should Zadie Smith worry that someone, somewhere, would prefer that she not base her novel *On Beauty* on a foundation drawn from Forster's *Howards End*? Why should Salman Rushdie not build into *The Satanic Verses* narrative elements taken from the Islamic tradition in order to create a world in which the supreme deity is both devil and god, "the Fellow Upstairs" and "the Guy from Underneath"? Surely Rankine knows as well as anyone else that there are potentially extraordinary advantages in refusing to "place" or settle for "limits."

That there may also be dangers entailed in sailing off into unknown waters is likewise obvious. But those are dangers any artist will confront, even when no appropriation of an alien perspective or cultural trope is involved. Rankine believes, in good faith, that she is warning against the predations of appropriation when it is "irresponsible," and yet in fact she offers no legitimate objection to appropriation itself, much though she seems to feel that her opposition is justified by the many instances she has witnessed of bad faith on the part of artists who do not adequately acknowledge what is problematic in their practice.

To say that art in general—all art—has inevitably to do with appropriation is to say what is clear to anyone who has made art and attempted to think about it. But it is also clear that certain kinds of art are more insistently rooted in appropriation than others. If we say "Eliot" and "The Waste Land," we know that we are speaking of appropriation in a sense utterly distinct from anything customarily observed in the work of most other poets. Manet's *Olympia* calls to mind a whole range of prototypes, borrowings, and allusions to "the tradition," in a way that diverges substantially from comparable paintings by other nineteenth-century artists. Each such instance raises questions about what and how the appropriations are managed. Each invites appraisal, comparison, and critical judgment. The issue is not whether or not Eliot or Manet should have been permitted to do what was done. We don't ask—ought not to ask—whether Eliot, as an American, or a white man, or a Christian, should have thought it legitimate to appropriate the language, the idiom, or the experience of persons not himself.

Of course scholars have long demonstrated that there is what the art historian Ingrid Rowland calls an "age-old interdependence of the European and Islamic worlds in a spirit of equality," and that in many places "the division between East and West has never been a real division." In the past, they note, "Arab mathematicians read the Greek philosophers eagerly, without worrying about Eurocentrism or colonialism or barriers of language." There is in our common history, if we would but yield to it, an "essential message: that human knowledge, and the human will to beauty, know no boundaries of time, space, or culture."

Suspicion is now the required posture toward those who wish to walk about under no one's surveillance.

And yet there remains, among the cultural guardians, a persisting tendency to suppress that message, to insist that division—along ethnic lines especially—is the essential truth, and to be savage toward artists who take liberties and fail to stand perpetual vigil over themselves. Fail to take due note of boundaries. Suspicion is now the required posture toward those who would wish to walk about under no one's surveillance. Appropriation thus occasionally understandable, even perhaps inevitable, but legitimate only if conforming to the proper spirit. A spirit cautious. Contrite. Sworn to do no harm. As if artists were not at least somewhat at the mercy of their desires and bound to revel in their wayward intensities.

In the essay "I Confess: My Cultural Misappropriation," Allan Gurganus—whose novel *Oldest Living Confederate Widow Tells All* is a classic work of appropriation—describes us as "an attractive string-pulling species that loves to make things" and will not be satisfied by a "one-voice one-note puppetry," each of us even as children "enlivening . . . inanimates," and in turn "being puppeteered by the dire need: to know what it meant to be a lion, a very old man, a powerfully beautiful woman." There are no guilty pleasures in this portrait, the relevant coordinates, in Gurganus's gorgeous telling, varieties of "depth and pity" in the maker's "consideration of others," so that, for this writer, "speaking as a Tyrolean wood cutter, or a pretty blond lady in red, taught me what I was—and was not. And was not yet." Though by no means cautious or contrite, Gurganus in fact proceeds as a writer in the spirit of a man with no instinct to do harm, to appall or offend. No respecter of boundaries, Gurganus takes liberties, but does so, as it were, always in the service of a vision capacious and scrupulous. Even his satire is essentially benevolent, an attempt to show us to ourselves as we are and to register the sometimes cruel power we exert. His appropriations need no apology, and thus it is not surprising that Toni Morrison celebrated them, praising the black character who speaks in *Confederate Widow* for "not having put a foot wrong in 718 pages," so that Gurganus "sobbed as only a liberal puppeteer probably should, even in private."

And in truth we want no less from those who appropriate—no less than depth and pity, and "consideration of others," and not putting "a foot wrong." Why not want that? Though there is, after all, another kind of virtue in another kind of work, conceived and executed by another kind of imagination. What to call this other kind of virtue? Call it, if you like, the virtue of not providing the very thing most of us continue to want. Call it the virtue of a considered perversity, the determined going against the grain of decency and benevolence. An accent there is, surely, that doesn't wish us well, an art that has no instinct for charity or homage. Philip Roth's character Mickey Sabbath, in the novel *Sabbath's Theater*, says, "My failure is failing to have gone far *enough*! My failure is not having gone *further*." Comparable assertions of appetite or unappeasable rage appear in a wide range of works, from the novels of Dostoyevsky and Thomas Bernhard to the dark fantasias of Georges Bataille. There is the libidinal overdrive of Anthony Burgess's novel *A Clockwork Orange*, where the target is the tendency of the state, the society, the established order, to seek to eliminate all propensities deemed dangerous, and with the dramatized consequence that things can go "too far," as Burgess himself has noted: "[The state] has entered a region," he writes, "beyond its covenant with the citizen," so that the novelist felt it his duty to say "that it is better to be bad of one's own free will than to be good through scientific brainwashing."

Not all of us will find this line of reasoning persuasive, even in works we find thrilling. But in closing these reflections I did want to say that the strain of perversity and indecency is some of the time present in the appropriations of artists and writers, and that we ought not to defend appropriation by pretending that, where it exists, it is invariably benevolent. There is no crime in appropriation per se, even where the scruple, benevolence, and humaneness of an Allan Gurganus are not at all in evidence.

To choose but a single example: the postmodern layerings and provocations that mark the work of the German painter Sigmar Polke are by no means uniformly benevolent. Often they feature borrowings and quotations selected to mock predecessors and to ridicule the sanctimony associated with artistic influence. The writing that celebrates Polke is typically riddled with words like "contamination" and "impurity," and emphatically underlines his determination to use his art to free himself from "misplaced or pernicious definitions of the proper and normal." In this sense, one outrageous aspect of Polke's appropriation is his use of the swastika, sometimes as a punk element, but also as part of an effort, by many German artists in Polke's postwar cohort, to "break [the] taboos" of an older generation. This, like other obscene gestures featured in Polke, is of course open to critique, but the critique ought to be focused on the use he made of the appropriated symbol, rather than on the fact that a particular artist dared to risk the appropriation, or transgressed merely by proceeding as if he was free to follow out the logic of his own creative idea. Perhaps, as the critic Kathy Halbreich suggested, Polke "sensed that [the] persistent vilification [of the swastika symbol] after the war had robbed it of some of its animating power, like an expletive repeated constantly, and thus felt almost obliged to use it," thereby preserving its horror, saving it "as an image that [had] become almost banal." This seems, in any case, a plausible way to explain the effect of an appropriation that will seem offensive to some viewers, and should, in any case, be debated in an environment that permits consideration of context, audience, and the status of "intention."

There is no formula that will justify absolutely anything an artist does. The instinct to go against the grain or break taboos may well be, in any particular instance, puerile, or betray an element of self-satisfaction, or seem to us irredeemably disgusting. Perversity is no more a guarantor of success—or even legitimacy—in art than moving accounts of altruism or political revolution, which are apt often to trade in sentimentalities and slogans. Appropriation is best regarded as a strategy that works or doesn't work, that justifies itself or fails to justify itself. It can be obvious or routine, an expression of respect or of vandalism. If we find it, *here*, or *here*, offensive, then we are obliged to make a case, to explain—to ourselves, at least— what has been sought and what has been wasted or demeaned. Categorical judgments based on a puerile notion of who owns what, or what must never be attempted, or what can never be tolerated, are inevitably driven by complacency.*

---

* In "Mixed Chorus," the poet Robert Pinsky pays homage to the virtues of "Creole," of mixing and borrowing, summoning, among others, the words of W. E. B. Du Bois, who likewise extolled the virtues of appropriation: "Across the color line I summon Aurelius," Pinsky's speaker says, "And Aristotle: threading through Philistine / And Amalekite they come, all graciously / And without condescension."

JUNK THOUGHT:
THE WAY WE LIVE NOW

The tigers of wrath are crossed with the horses of instruction.

—Saul Bellow

Outside a small gallery in Rome, just around the corner from Piazza Navona, Peg Boyers and I stopped to look through the window at a painting. The scene a jazz club, the characters black, the most prominent among them a dancing and singing young woman in a state of undress, others peeking out from behind a curtain or reaching for a drink. The architecture of the canvas impressively bold, the action nicely captured, the surface crowded but dynamic, all of it in a period style that has "Jazz Age" written all over it, while also betraying the influence of a pop-cubism keyed to fragmented views and facet line divisions. Another feature: the words "Hot Chocolates" skillfully set across one side of the painting. When we entered the gallery we were told that the painting, dated 1928, was by the German artist Winold Reiss, who had spent much of his life in the United States. Later, after consulting with our youngest son, Gabe, an art dealer in Boston, we learned that the work in question was actually a copy of a well-known Reiss painting celebrating the Fats Waller musical revue *Hot Chocolates*, which had featured, among other performers, the young Louis Armstrong. The painting had been reproduced in numbers of books on the Harlem Renaissance.

Though the Rome gallerist knew very little about this background, he did speculate that the painting was probably a commissioned work, no doubt intended to be hung in the nightclub itself.

Soon we left Rome but found ourselves thinking again about *Hot Chocolates* and, more especially, about responses to it by people to whom we'd sent a photo of the thing. The most troubling feature of the work—especially if you know nothing about its provenance—is its title, painted across the surface of the painting. The words "Hot Chocolates" carried with them an obviously racialist, if not overtly racist, suggestion, proposing that the black women depicted in the painting be regarded—in the language now very familiar in race studies—as commodified bodies. Though there is nothing grossly carnal or appetitive in Reiss's figures, who are depicted in outline, almost as in a poster illustration, with big eyes and seductively sinuous bodies, the atmosphere of the work is enticingly sexualized. In many ways the scene, as depicted, resembles the images displayed on dozens, if not hundreds, of old album or sheet music covers. Such images were used as promotional materials, and a great many of them are the products of black artists and designers. Absurd, of course, to think of these kinds of images as "innocent," and yet they convey no trace of derision or malice. The figures belong to a scene in which they are permitted to play and be joyous. We are not invited, as onlookers, to ask questions about where they come from or what has brought them to such a place. The standard language nowadays used to deplore the commodification of black bodies is both poignant and, as applied to the Reiss painting, misplaced.

And still, as I say, there was something troubling about the image. Knowing what we know about the uses to which black bodies have been subjected, we cannot but feel at least a certain unease when we find ourselves responding with unforced pleasure to such a depiction—particularly when the words "Hot Chocolates" are used as a prompt to signal lascivious intent. To anyone for whom "naughty" or "seductive" suggests violation, of course, the mere sight of a naked young woman dancing joyously and kicking up her proverbial heels is bound to provoke discomfort or opprobrium. But then, the scene filled me and my wife with a desire to be there in that club and to get up and dance to the music of Fats Waller, whose naughty lyrics we sing to each other all the time. This was, after all, the universe that, in the 1920s and 1930s, gave us "Ain't Misbehavin'," "Honeysuckle Rose," and "Don't Let It Bother You," and there was nothing in the Reiss painting that betrayed any sentiment or suggestion that was incompatible with the spirit of Waller's often provocative lyrics. If we were troubled, a little, that seemed very much in keeping with what we usually want from a work of art, that it seem not quite digestible, not quite the delightful and uncomplicated surface that at first draws our attention. Was there not, in Reiss's naughty figures, an invitation to take in the scene with something more than a laugh and a shrug?

Of course the images in Reiss's painting are one-dimensional. A friend to whom we sent a photograph of the painting called them "lewd caricatures," though again I insist that they aren't gross or salacious, the images so frankly playful and gestural as to dispel any complaint that they are merely one-dimensional. Caricatures? I don't think so. One-dimensional only in the sense that the figures are types set in a characteristic milieu to which they inevitably belong. To demand of such a work that it deliver what it was not intended to deliver is a category error, somewhat like demanding that an autumn landscape manage to avoid russet browns or the red wash spreading over distant hills, or that a prose passage evoking an industrial waste site not convey the acid smell of gas refineries. On the evidence of *Hot Chocolates*, Reiss seems to have understood perfectly what Fats Waller himself had in mind for his musical revue, and the lewdness, such as it is, is fully in keeping with the spirit of comically leering, ironic insouciance that marks a Waller lyric.

And why does this matter? It matters because we are, all of us, deeply worried. We have been turned into consumers (and also artists and writers) with a very bad conscience. Worried that we will disappoint someone's expectations about what we like and ought to like. Fluent with anxiety about art that offends, that fails not to take the essential steps to guard against being misunderstood. Ready, all too ready, to back away from works that could conceivably seem to someone to carry a taint. Wanting to read books as if they appealed to us only for the right reasons, and to promote or purchase only artworks that are forthright in their affirmation of the good and the safe. My American friend who responded to the email attachment of the Reiss painting first with disdain and then with fear and trembling—"You're not seriously thinking of buying it and putting that painting up in your house, are you?"—knew all too well what "someone" was apt to believe about us if we were foolish enough to hang the thing on our living room wall.

But then, this whole business matters also because we have grown confused about what we value in artworks and books. The Reiss painting looks "dangerous" because we're not sure that the painter was himself alert to "commodification" or to the prospect that someone would get the wrong idea about a musical revue trading in black bodies and deliriously rambunctious sexual innuendo. We want to believe that we're not susceptible to humorless, simpleminded notions that forbid sexual tease and unsolemn libidinous play, even as we struggle to find ways to deal with our fear that we will fail to be properly offended. We tell ourselves that we will not be readily scandalized by a careless Balthus adolescent or a slyly suggestive lyric, that we will read the way we're supposed to read, giving ourselves freely into the hands of artists, allowing books not to be soothing or correct. That, at least, is what we tell ourselves. And yet more and more many of us demand—for example, of the books in our hands— that they deliver only what such books are supposed to say, as if we were waiting for a stamped and posted package of reliably sanitized goods pitched and addressed to the right-minded likes of us. Often we are impatient with ambiguity and positively uncomfortable with irony. We want benevolent sentiments underlined, nastiness and predation fenced off and labeled. We want to have fun, but only if it's an approved sort of fun. Tame. Terribly decent.

In several respects these developments reflect the relentless politicization of art and literature in the culture. Of course politicization is nothing new. It's obvious that power, class, gender, race, and entitlement have at least something to do with our responses to books and artworks. Often ideology has shaped, even dictated, opinion in the arts. And yet what is taking shape right now is driven by a species of ideology that is most often unacknowledged, and pernicious precisely because its contours are ill defined. Reviewers, even at the major newspapers, often write as undisguised cheerleaders primed to applaud artworks, poetry, and fiction principally for their espousal of widely accredited views that are underwritten by ideas they themselves would be hard put to articulate or name. They are in thrall to an ideological cast of mind even while supposing that ideology has nothing whatever to do with their disposition. Many writers stand ready to affirm primarily what is certain to win instant approval, and are encouraged—by editors and other enthusiasts—to come out with empty affirmations of the current line on everything from "power" to "authority."

Students are often bright and inquiring, but a good part of what they learn from their most influential teachers is what not to ask.

Not long ago it was only right-wing polemicists like Norman Podhoretz, Hilton Kramer, and Roger Kimball who routinely came out with pontifications notable for the high proportion of willful misrepresentation they contained. But in the academy and in influential quarters of the literary world the will to differentiate a palpable untruth from a plausible statement is increasingly rare. Young people in the colleges and universities are often bright and inquiring, but a good part of what they learn from their most influential teachers and role models is what not to ask. The demand for "safety" clearly entails knowing what is off-limits, and what is off-limits is what requires that the students and their enablers ask uncomfortable questions more than they would ever hope to do.

Consider the provocation represented by a recent essay published in the *New York Times Book Review.* "Provocation" as in "that which must be responded to," though the readership was, so far as I can tell, not much provoked. The essay, by the Pulitzer Prize–winning novelist Viet Thanh Nguyen, was entitled "How Writers' Workshops Can Be Hostile." The palpable motives for the essay: Grievance. The desire to invoke familiar noise words ("power," "theory," "hostile") without having to explain or earn them. The setting up of an "us versus them" in which THEY (white people who exercise the ostensibly immense powers invested in writing programs) operate with "unexamined assumptions" and WE (the poor immigrant wretches who win scholarships and fellowships to study in those writing programs) "come bearing the experiences and ideas the workshop suppresses." The language is telling. Not experiences and ideas that are *ignored* but *suppressed.* Not "theory" as in a *particular* theory but simply "theory." Not "power" as in *which* power specifically but simply "power." Not "suppresses" as in suppresses *how, when,* and *where* but simply "suppresses." Not "hostile" as in hostility expressed in *what form,* under *which auspices,* but simply "hostile." The fact that this essay could be published in the pages of the *New York Times Book Review* says a good deal about the state of the culture and about misleading assertions against which many students who admire writers like Nguyen are bound to be defenseless. How to resist the polemic of a writer whose family had to flee Vietnam during the fall of Saigon in 1975 and whose first novel has won major prizes, richly deserved? How to summon the critical spirit to think, really think, about what has been said when the will to invest in the stock scenario—the powerful suppress the weak, the insiders are hostile to the outsiders, THEY are not adequately interested in US—is apt to be overmastering?

The Nguyen essay purports to give us "an object lesson in how power propagates and conceals itself." The power here has to do with what Nguyen regards as the awful conspiracy of those who teach in writing programs to make persons like himself—"women and people of color"—feel that they are in "hostile" territory. Never mind that a very large proportion of the people enrolled in writing programs, all across the country, are women. Never mind that in the best writing programs a great many of those enrolled are on generous fellowships and that many of those enrolled are in fact people of color. Forget about the fact that women writers are very well represented on the faculties of writing programs. Never mind that in programs like my own New York State Summer Writers Institute, which I founded more than thirty years ago, more than a third of the sixty-five scholarships given to students in 2018 went to people of color. Or that the teaching faculty and visiting writers rosters have always contained at least as many women as men. Nguyen clearly has failed to do his homework, and thus "propagates" a series of falsehoods that serve to prop up an argument he is determined to wage—an argument that many in the academy and in the literary culture wish to swallow and pass along.

But Nguyen's argument is telling in many other respects as well. After all, he informs us, in writing programs people like himself have reason to be "worried that my historical and political concerns . . . wouldn't find a receptive audience." Why not? Obviously—this is the way Nguyen thinks about such matters—persons who do not come from his country, who do not share his background, will simply not be interested in what he has to say. Here is a writer who apparently doesn't believe that other writers—who have long taught in writing programs—often write about persons and places and histories that do not belong to them. Who can't acknowledge that Russell Banks, a white man, can write novels about the "historical and political concerns" of people who live in Liberia, Jamaica, and other locations outside his native New Hampshire. Who must be astonished to learn that Carolyn Forché, a white midwesterner with Czech origins, writes passionately about people in El Salvador and brings out popular anthologies introducing American workshop students to the poetry produced by writers from all over the world. Who doesn't quite accept that many writers are more interested in what is unfamiliar than in what is familiar, and that when they write about the familiar they labor to make it unfamiliar. Why, Nguyen

asks, would the kinds of white people who teach in writing programs, committed as they are to the "defense of the individual and
his humanistic expression," find themselves drawn to the subject
of "politics and the spirit of collectives"—thereby suggesting that
there is an unbridgeable gap between a "defense of the individual"
and an interest in those other important matters that, presumably,
only persons like himself can handle. Underwriting Nguyen's essay
is an unbecoming narcissism and an exotic species of chauvinism
according to which only people accustomed to thinking of themselves as "other" can conceivably be interested in what really matters.

A young person eager to drink at this well of misinformation and
grievance, inclined to be moved by Nguyen's reference to people like
himself as "the barbarians at the gate," will inevitably be inclined
to believe him when he writes that "the workshop reproduces its
ideology," encourages only "a particular kind of writing," is "the
expression of . . . the white majority," and is bound to suppress "our
stories." What, I wonder, is the "ideology" that aptly and coherently
describes the perspective of all or most workshop teachers? Do Rivka
Galchen and Joyce Carol Oates share a particular ideology? Jorie
Graham and Louise Glück? Are minority writers who teach creative
writing bound to promote a particular ideology? Caryl Phillips and
Gregory Pardlo, Margo Jefferson and Danzy Senna: all of them one
voice, one story, one set of prescriptions? Consider that the workshop
Nguyen describes in these terms is not an ideological formation or
abstraction but the classrooms of the teachers who have instructed
and worked with generations of students in writers workshops—the
classrooms of Ann Beattie and Francine Prose, Mary Gaitskill and
Allan Gurganus, Robert Coover, Marilynne Robinson, and dozens
of others. What—again I ask—is the "ideology" that is uniformly
propagated by all of these writers, white or black, Asian or Latino?

What is the "particular kind of writing" propagated by Frank Bidart and Vijay Seshadri, Tobias Wolff and the late Bharati Mukherjee? Which stories have been suppressed by which of these writers? Why does an essay purporting to know something not name names?

The assertions that fuel these questions are so without foundation as to indicate, once more, that we are observing, all across the culture, the rise of what Susan Jacoby calls "junk thought." Previously we had thought this the province principally of "right-wing politicians and commentators," who mock "any scientific consensus that contradicts their political, economic, or cultural agenda" or conduct arguments with "a tenuous or nonexistent relationship to evidence." Jacoby argues that junk thought has "gained social respectability . . . during the past half century," and "that it interacts toxically with the most credulous elements in both secular and religious ideologies." One alarming fact, Jacoby notes, is that junk thought "is often employed by highly intelligent people"—Nguyen is a perfect example—who deploy language to promote ideas that have little or no relation to the reality they purport to describe. This, alas, is increasingly prevalent in academic communities, where the rage to get on the ostensible right side of certain issues and to deny inconvenient truths has made performances like Nguyen's all too common.

Again, the really disheartening feature of this situation is that the platitudes and formulas that mark Nguyen's essay have had their way, not only with a great many students, but with the rest of us, including those of us who are not credulous but find it difficult to tell students how hard it will be for them not to be violated by ideas. When I hear a student trot out some version of the thing Nguyen and others like him are hawking, I invariably invite the student to my office for a long conversation—the kind of conversation I would dearly like to conduct one day with Nguyen himself. But then, students are deeply reluctant to give up even the most egregious and insupportable formulas, and find that a great many of their teachers are likewise fond of them. Jacoby details cases of "intellectual quackery" among academics in departments of philosophy, musicology, women's studies, economics, and neurology, and it is clear that the very prospect of thinking clearly—with a respect for ordinary standards of evidence and logic—about complex issues is now virtually impossible for a great many people in academic life.

That the situation is especially dire just about any classroom teacher with years of experience in the contemporary university will concede. I know there is a danger in thinking about the present situation as if there had been in the past a golden age, when politics did not occupy our thoughts quite so insistently, and students were more willing than they are at present to cut their professors some slack and not be waiting for them to misstep and thereby demonstrate their cluelessness about "power" and the creation of "hostile" environments.* Even those of us who are old enough to remember a time when teachers and students were not perpetually congratulating themselves on the perfection of their responses to everything under

---

* The readiness to punish alleged miscreants takes many forms. In an essay on "Puritans and Prigs," Marilynne Robinson speaks of the widespread addiction to postures of rectitude, the readiness to rebuke "forbidden words" that carry no "hint of aspersion" in them. "No matter," Robinson writes, "that the man who mis-spoke is known to be a very generous-spirited man . . . Social methods that have been used to restrict the expression of obscenity or aggression, shaming, for example, are slurring over to control many other forms of language." Those who are in the vanguard of the thought reform promoted along these lines, Robinson goes on, "can only experience virtuousness as difference," "do not really want to enlist or persuade," and behave in accordance with "the operations of simple [ideological] fashion."

the sun do now accept that there were all sorts of things we might have noticed back in those palmier days. We recall the so-called canon wars that roiled the campuses thirty years ago, and we can allow ourselves to be grateful that we were forced to revisit the whole idea of the canon and to figure out ways to open it up—though of course there were losses involved in that process, losses that faculty and students are not only ill equipped to think about but positively unwilling even to acknowledge. Such as? Such as the notion that, in the realm of academic study, "choice" is not invariably a right or a principle that we ought to champion. Or such as the notion that it may really be beneficial for students to have a command of the history of a genre before engaging in advanced literary study. Or the notion that some books, by virtue of the influence they exerted on generations of artists or writers or scholars, really are more important for students to read than others. These are only a few of the issues that were debated during the period of the canon wars, and though no one now believes that those wars can or should be fought again, it is worth noting that the failure to acknowledge what happened in the course of those wars, or to register what really were significant losses, is part of the general mood of denial that grips the academy.

But there are many kinds of denial, and those of us who are adept at anatomizing the varieties of denial that have brought us the presidency of Donald Trump—not to mention the idiocies promoted by the American evangelical Right or the malignant deceits promoted by the Republican Party and its elected officials—might well also note, more than we are inclined to do, the denial we routinely practice in our roles as critics and teachers. Denials that affect what we teach, what we demand, how we respond to an environment that is increasingly intolerant and illiberal. Denials that also infect our habits as readers, as persons entrusted with the education of students, whose instincts are being shaped by assumptions they are urged not to interrogate or push back against. "What counts as an accurate report of experience," the philosopher Richard Rorty wrote some years ago, "is a matter of what a community will let you get away with." A community that is willing to let a writer like Viet Thanh Nguyen get away with obvious distortion and misinformation is a community in trouble. In the classroom the tendency to denial would include the willingness, on the part of a faculty member, to let an obvious misstatement or distortion of fact go unchallenged—often for fear of introducing a factor, or a fact, that would decidedly complicate the trajectory of an ongoing discussion. Such as? Such as the fact that a plausible narrative is not actually as simple and pleasing as we had wanted it to be. Say that in a seminar in Twentieth-Century American Poetry, a student has just made a compelling and credible case, arguing that women poets have been consistently discriminated against by male writers and critics in the literary establishment and that their voices until quite recently had been suppressed. Would the instructor in such a seminar, presumably learned about such matters, congratulate the student for the cogency of her presentation, agree that there is much to be learned from her research, and then go on to note that in fact the story is rather more complicated? That, say, male poets and critics—Robert Lowell, W. H. Auden, Randall Jarrell, A. Alvarez, Hayden Carruth, many others—had vigorously promoted the works of writers like Marianne Moore, Adrienne Rich, Elizabeth Bishop, Anne Sexton, Sylvia Plath, and other brilliant women: reviewing their works in prominent periodicals, awarding them prizes, and so on? That a woman named Louise Bogan was for more than forty years the poetry editor of the *New Yorker*? Or would it now seem the better part of valor not to go on to mention such facts, in the interests of allowing everyone in the class to relax into a more consoling and familiar sort of narrative? Underlying that familiar narrative is a truth—the long, ugly history of sexism that we now fortunately know a great deal about. But we do want also to know that even such a history contains, though all too rarely, unexpected features.

Last year I taught Ian McEwan's novel *On Chesil Beach*, in which a disastrous opening night of a marriage destroys the lives of husband and wife, both of them sexually inept, the wife clearly and pathologically revolted by sexual contact of any kind, the husband stunned by the wife's display of revulsion and unable to recover from the bitterness unleashed in the course of this unforgettable encounter. McEwan handles the material in the novel so deftly and compassionately that it seemed impossible—to me, at any rate—to suppose that anyone but the husband and wife of the disastrous marriage would think to assign blame to either party. Though the wife's revulsion is somewhat accounted for in terms of her background—there is an ambiguous suggestion that she might have suffered some early sexual trauma, perhaps even experienced some form of abuse—nothing is made to line up exactly, and we are permitted to feel both that the wife's behavior is pathological, inordinate, and also that she is to be pitied and by no means condemned. Just so, though we can see that the husband might well have responded to his wife's display of revulsion and her barrage of verbal abuse in a more forgiving way, we can also see that he did nothing to deserve our contempt. McEwan ensures that, whatever the two principal figures make of what they have been through, we will find them human, all too human, perhaps ill at ease with our recourse to a term like "pathological" to describe the wife's behavior, and uncomfortable thinking that the husband was somehow blameworthy by virtue of his failure to be exemplary.

In my class—an advanced class, consisting largely of English majors, most of whom had studied with me previously in other courses—I was dismayed that a good many of the students insisted that of course the husband was to blame for what had happened. Women, after all, so it was explained, had good reason to be unprepared for what was to befall them on a wedding night in a period—McEwan had made it perfectly clear that this series of events took place just before the advent of the 1960s sexual revolution—when men were apt not to be sufficiently sensitive to their fears, and women would typically have no prior experience of sex. This sense of the thing was articulated by virtually all of the young women enrolled in the class, and if any of

Blame was what my students mainly wanted to hold on to, given that blame is always bound to simplify one's understanding.

the male students were inclined to dispute it, they certainly did not speak up to say so. And though I patiently took the class through the passages of the novel that would seem to make the whole idea of blaming either of these characters for what had happened impossible, I left with the unmistakable impression that blame was what my students mainly wanted to hold on to, given that blame is always bound to simplify one's understanding of a conflict—also given the fact that, where conflicts involving men and women are at issue, the default position is now to feel that the system is such that even apparently sympathetic male characters cannot be blameless. What I witnessed, in other words, was the operation of a fairly elementary set of assumptions and instincts that will not be easy to dislodge. Nor will it be easy to think of the reading habits associated with these assumptions as anything but unfortunate.

And speaking of reading habits and assumptions, consider a novel called *The Woman Upstairs* (2013) by Claire Messud—a novel I've been teaching for five years. At its center is a woman bitter about her failings and her failures, a woman in early middle age who has had advantages—a decent education, a decent job, the admiration of those with whom she is routinely involved, loving and supportive parents—but finds herself envying the drive and success of others. A woman who thinks of most other persons as "mediocre"—her word—and believes that women especially have long suffered as a result of their inadequate ambition, their willingness to acknowledge their own limitations, and most especially their refusal to get angry, really angry.

Bitterness is of course a sentiment often sounded by many different kinds of characters who lament the life not lived, opportunities missed, structural inequalities that favor the chances of the privileged. But Messud's character Nora often makes her case in gender terms. She hates the fact that she is and has been what she calls "a dutiful daughter." Emphasis on both terms, "dutiful" and "daughter." She hates the fact that her own mother lived what was apparently a contented life and never clamored for one of those "volcanic eruptions" that can shake and transform a world. "I wanted—I needed—her to revolt," Nora reflects, hating that her mother found a way "to accept her modest share." Modesty seems to Messud's character a form of dreadful failure, a form—so she believes—embraced by generations of women and still, in the twenty-first century, the terrible fate even of women who have jobs they like and little apparent reason to blame circumstance or biology or men for the shape of their lives. Confronting the fact that she never pursued her art after graduating from art school, Nora indulges the thought that her failure has much or everything to do with the indisputable fact that she is and has been a woman. Why? Because women simply are not good at asserting and insisting on their desires. They don't know how to say no to suffering or to turn their backs on arrangements that they dislike. No more now than, say, fifty or sixty years ago. Whereas "men have generations of practice at this," Nora believes, and "have figured out how to spawn children and leave them to others to raise," women have not learned how to be strong. "You need," Nora declares, "to see everything else—everyone else—as expendable, as less than yourself."

The Woman Upstairs is by no means conceived as a political novel. It makes no reference to political or social movements. It is not invested in ideas of a world more attractive. It does not assemble characters to argue or debate political issues, and gives no consideration to the way strong-minded or otherwise powerful individuals mobilize others to effect change. It is a first-person novel with an intense and unyielding focus on the unfolding consciousness of a character in crisis, one who has no inclination to concern herself with the woes or the prospects of others, however much she rails bitterly about the lot of women. And though this character speaks with enormous ferocity and knows how to articulate a litany of pointed complaints, her bitterness is so comprehensive, her resentments so sweeping and indiscriminate, that it is impossible to regard her as the source of a reliably informed or coherent political critique.

Disappointing, then, that many readers of Messud's novel have largely misread the book and its intentions, and yet also not at all surprising, given those habits and assumptions we've cited. Daphne Merkin tells us that the novel "takes on, at full throttle, the ways in which women are socialized into being accommodating 'nice girls.'" It is even—"it may well be," she says—"the first truly feminist (in the best, least didactic sense) novel I have read in ages." Others, like the critic Ron Charles, are excited about the "rich veins of indignation" the novel exposes and regard Nora's anger as an expression of Messud's "reaction to persistent social inequality." Persistent. As if nothing much has changed in the last few decades. Even readers who are properly turned off by Nora—by her unearned sense of entitlement, her inability to acknowledge that she is the source of her own disappointment, not to mention her envy of other women who have made art and created families and done their work without compulsively comparing their lot to the charmed lives of others— tend to read Nora as something of a stand-in for her author. "For Nora, and, one gathers, for Messud," writes Emily Witt in what is a characteristic misreading of *The Woman Upstairs*. Leave aside the fact that Claire Messud is a successful, acclaimed, highly productive woman writer with access to the pages of the most influential magazines in the country. By no means a woman who could conceivably complain that she has been overlooked or condescended to or that she has been the victim of "persistent social inequality." Consider instead that Messud has brilliantly given voice to a character who has not even tried to do the exalted artistic work she thinks she was meant to do, and believes that—as Witt has it—"a median salary and a job well done as, say, a teacher, are the marks of . . . failure."

To be sure, Messud's Nora is bound to seem to all of us a familiar figure and to seem, in obvious ways, to speak for disappointments and failures we know all too well, no matter how invested we are in the work we have chosen to do. Messud says in an interview that "she's an amalgam of myself, people I've known, stories I've heard," and that certainly seems fair and plausible enough. Who—man or woman—hasn't been now and then susceptible to a modicum at least of bitterness and envy? Who hasn't been inclined, occasionally, to blame on circumstance or inequality or sexism or race prejudice or political correctness failures better regarded as the luck of the draw or a reflection of our own deep limitations? Not so very long ago it was entirely reasonable to think that, no matter what a woman might do or create, her gender would prevent her from receiving her due or close off opportunities that men might well take for granted. But Messud puts things perfectly when she says of Nora that, in her "rant, she puts herself in a feminist context, if you will, when in fact her primary concern is herself and her own story." Exactly. "To the extent," Messud goes on, "that we have a political consciousness, it does relate to us, to our own experiences." But that very "political consciousness" is apt, here and in many other cases, to mislead—in this case, to tempt a reader of a novel like *The Woman Upstairs* to forget that Nora's "primary concern is herself and her own story," and that the story she tells about her life is distorted by her deep, unacknowledged suspicion that—as another writer has said—"she has sabotaged her own artistic ambition."

Political consciousness is, in many respects, a good and desirable thing. Obvious but true. But equally true is the fact—and it is a fact— that ideas play a notable part in the formation of a so-called political consciousness, and that the mind often finds itself defenseless against appealing ideas. Readers of novels with ostensive political implications are especially vulnerable to the species of corruption famously captured by T. S. Eliot when he spoke of a mind that can be "violated by an idea." Messud's Nora is just such a character in the sense that she exhibits the will to apply to her own situation ideas associated with feminist militancy when in truth those ideas have virtually nothing—so far as we can tell from Nora's first-person account—to do with the deficits she confronts. Not to be able to read Messud's novel with a clear sense that Nora is a classic case of an unreliable narrator is not to be able to read very well. And the will to misread such a work reflects an unfortunate disposition to hold on to what are by now dubious assumptions still routinely validated by the zeitgeist. To be violated by ideas, and to deny that this is so, is very much a feature of our current situation. Messud's Nora is an object lesson in that species of violation.

The rage to reduce a given novel to message, to assign it a definite purpose, is of a piece with the desire to insist on its directness and transparency. The structural and rhetorical devices employed by a first-rate writer like Messud are designed to ensure that her plots and characters will not be made into one-dimensional outlines and readily exploited. And yet everywhere, among reviewers, academics, and students, there is the demand for ideological transparency, and everywhere we are uneasy lest we disappoint the heavy expectations under which we conduct ourselves as readers and writers.

Toni Morrison has famously spoken and written about the virtues of "playing in the dark," and that would seem a necessary recommendation. To play in the dark, as Teju Cole has suggested, is to preserve some possibility of "opacity," "obscurity," and "inscrutability." Not to make a fetish of obscurity but to resist whatever it is in "mainstream culture" that would have us, as readers, as makers, play to expectations. Cole speaks of the philosopher Édouard Glissant, who sought in his work to expose the "external pressures [that] insisted on everything being illuminated, simplified and explained," to which he offered a "gentle refusal," a simple "no." That simple "no" is what we will need to summon as we confront the "external pressures" to give the thought police—in classrooms, academic departments, editorial offices—exactly what they think they want from us and from the books and artworks we confront.

EPILOGUE:
WHAT IS TO BE DONE?

The last mass trials were a great success. There are going to be fewer but better Russians.

—Ernst Lubitsch, *Ninotchka*

The stories I have told in this book do not provide a strong empirical case for optimism. In several respects the tendencies that alarmed many of us on the liberal Left twenty-five or thirty years ago have grown more disturbing. Intolerance among young people and their academic sponsors in the university is more entrenched than it was before, and both administrators and a large proportion of the liberal professoriate are running scared, fearful that they will be accused of thought crimes if they speak out against even the most obvious abuses and absurdities. An Ivy League college senior, enrolled in my July 2018 New York State Summer Writers Institute, told me that in his workshop he was denounced by several other students for writing poems that draw on his experience working as a volunteer in Bryan Stevenson's Equal Justice Initiative in Alabama. How dare he write poems about lynching and the travails of oppressed people when it was obvious that he has no legitimate claim to that material? Was it not obvious that a "privileged" white male, who could afford to take off a year of college to work as a volunteer, really had no access to the sufferings of the people he hoped to study and evoke? It was not his poems that were intrinsically objectionable but his presumption in thinking himself entitled to write them. Though I assured the young man that his experience was not unusual, and that the students who attempted, in effect, to dictate to him the terms under which he might continue to write his poems belong to a powerful and deeply illiberal movement, he rightly observed that those students continue to think of themselves as social justice warriors, and believe that they are protecting people like their classmate from the ostracism and isolation that

It's tempting to speculate that liberalism has only itself to blame for the toxic environment that now permeates the liberal academy.

await him should he continue in his nefarious ways. The revolution of moral concern, driven by people in the grip of delusions I have attempted to anatomize throughout this book,* is clearly a bizarre phenomenon, fueled by convictions and passions that have the appearance of benevolence but are increasingly harnessed to create a surveillance culture in which strict adherence to irrational codes and "principles" is demanded.

---

* A controversy unfolded in July 2018 when the *Nation* magazine published a short poem by a young white poet who had dared to use black vernacular language in his poem. Online protest letters were predictably nasty and belligerent. Within a few days the poetry editors who had accepted the poem issued what *Nation* columnist Katha Pollitt called a "craven apology" which read "like a letter from a re-education camp." Among my own poet friends there were differences as to the merits of the poem. None thought it in the least offensive. In the *Atlantic*, the scholar of black English John McWhorter noted that the language of the poem was in fact "true and ordinary black speech" and a "spot-on depiction of the dialect in use." He also noted that, at a time when whites are encouraged "to understand . . . the black experience," white artists who seek "to empathize . . . as artists" are told to cease and desist. "Stay in your lane," commanded the writer Roxane Gay, who perhaps has not adequately thought through what is potentially entailed in that decree.

It's tempting to speculate that liberalism has only itself to blame for the toxic environment that now permeates the liberal academy. After all, liberals like myself long supposed that our commitment to more or less unrestricted free speech, candor, and openness was underwritten by a consensually agreed-on set of natural constraints. We could celebrate the distribution of disturbing, even pornographic books because we believed that somehow society would provide common standards of decency and misgiving that would prevent disturbing works from too entirely having their way with us. We could indulge in confrontational political demonstrations, burn our draft cards, and work in resistance organizations while continuing to believe not only that our goals were legitimate but that liberalism itself underwrote the challenge to the established order. But it has gradually become clear to us that we took rather too much for granted. Society provides very little in the way of common standards of decency or constraint. The internet empowers vast numbers of people to enact their worst selves and to participate in grotesque campaigns of slander, vilification, and irrationality. Where the political Right has Fox News to purvey lies, misinformation, and sheer ignorance, the liberal Left has drifted far from what had once seemed its inveterate willingness to acknowledge contradiction and to honestly tackle problems and deceits of its own devising. In many quarters we are now haunted by the specter of a liberalism increasingly drawn to denial and overt repression. Academic liberals who would have laughed thirty or forty years ago at the prospect of speech codes and draconian punishments for verbal indecorum or "presumption" are now not only compliant but enthusiastic about efforts to enforce standards many of them know to be intellectually indefensible. Those of us who are determined to call what is happening by its rightful name are astonished, again and again, by the virulence of efforts to deny what is now unmistakable.

It has never been so very easy for some of us to regard ourselves as liberals. When I was young I was drawn, like many others of my 1960s generation, to words like "revolution" and "liberation," and thought of liberals—Left liberals like myself included—as incorrigibly reasonable, well-meaning, and, even in our militancies, thoroughly uninspiring. Of course these sentiments were rooted in clichés and stereotypes, though we told ourselves that those very clichés were often accurate and had much besides to recommend them. Soon, however, I began to suspect that, whatever the demerits, timidities, and mild decencies of liberals, there was one thing above all that conferred dignity on our kind. We were, after all, routinely subjected to caricature and attack by people on the right and on the left. Our capacity for self-interrogation was derided as a form of self-debasement, our inclination to a yes-but form of argument as a sign of timidity or irresolution. We were said often to want to remain out of the line of fire, to occupy a center that was ideologically neutral. And yet we came increasingly to understand that we were, at our best, by no means neutral, and that in fact there was no center to occupy. The so-called center was a fiction summoned by generations of radicals of the left and right to differentiate themselves from persons without their furious certainties and their willingness to strike fear into the hearts of their adversaries. "What so infuriates opponents on left and right," writes Jonathan Freedland, "is the insistence that two things, usually held to be in opposition, can both be true." Uneasy,

> *It is decidedly* not *true that academics mobilizing to punish dissident voices on campuses are nevertheless operating with benevolent motives.*

to be sure, that insistence, not always perfectly defensible, and not always legitimate. Not all things "usually held to be in opposition" are both true. It is decidedly *not* true that academics mobilizing to punish dissident or "incorrect" voices on their own campuses are nevertheless operating with benevolent motives. It is *not* true that an ostensibly well-intentioned effort to prevent a young white poet from imagining the lives of black people is an expression of genuine concern for black people. There is no decent "center" where such issues are involved, no "both true," and it is part of the business of this book to argue precisely that. To be liberal is not to back down or back away. I so declare, even as a great many of those in my own cohort quietly, quiescently line up behind the cadres of those determined to create an environment largely populated by the cowed and compliant.

Of course there really are important things, "usually held to be in opposition," that "can both be true." And of course it has always been the work of intellectuals to identify opposing propositions or facts and to make the case for their "truth." In the course of this book I have tried to evoke such things. To argue that the idea of "privilege" has its important uses and is, at the same time, susceptible to misunderstanding and abuse. To demonstrate that the idea of "appropriation" was an understandable expression of legitimate and deep-seated fears held by people with a history of oppression and subordination, but that the idea soon came to be wielded by people ignorant of the ways of the imagination and the benefits of the very practices they resisted. To argue that "identity" is an important aspect of our ongoing efforts to understand ourselves, but that identity politics is based on a deep misunderstanding of the nature of race and ethnicity. To insist that policies like affirmative action are essential if we are ever to achieve the kind of social justice we aspire to but that there are costs and consequences we ought to acknowledge without pretending that those costs are negligible or incidental.

These and other such arguments, where apparently opposing ideas are shown to be "true," are bound to be attacked by proponents of the left and the right, and the environment thereby generated by such attacks will be vital or poisonous, depending on the range of factors cited in the pages of this book. Émile Zola, in his open letters to the youth of France, spoke of the "idiotic poison [that had] already overthrown their intellects." He was speaking of anti-Semitism and other features of the "sick moral atmosphere" gradually ascendant in the culture of late-nineteenth-century France. But Zola might well have been speaking instead of conditions now gradually ascendant in our own culture, where—in much of the academy—"no one dares say what he thinks for fear of being denounced" and public opinion, certainly as regards matters cultural and academic, is in the grip of a "somber obstinacy." Obstinacy in what sense? In the sense that what ought to be obvious is rigorously denied, and the consequence entailed in the creation of a campus culture marked by suspicion and intimidation is routinely dismissed as collateral damage.

I am aware that the words "no one dares say what he thinks for fear of being denounced" would seem to contradict the suggestion that intellectuals and students are vigorously marching in lockstep and fully at one with the nonsense peddled in seminars and in online forums. But this is another of those cases in which two apparently opposing things happen also both to be true. Many students and professors are in fact inflamed with the need to hunt out heretics and to extinguish all signs of "incorrect" or "uncomfortable" thinking. But even among the ideologically inflamed there are misgivings that they dare not acknowledge even to themselves. More important, though the majority of students and professors know very well that the present commitment to extinguish discomfort and to create an environment completely "safe" is not only hopeless but inimical to the goals of education, they also know very well that they had better not say what they think, while assuring themselves that their own misgivings are, after all, not terribly momentous.

Many of us are routinely moved by the dignity of our distress. Distress by no means limited to what confronts us in the course of an ordinary workday. We speak with undisguised outrage and conviction of the flagrant dishonesty and corruption of Washington elites, and assure one another that if things continue to unfold the way they have in recent years—most especially since the election of Donald Trump in 2016—we'll pack up and move to another country. New events, as they are brought to our attention, routinely crystallize our sense that we are living in the worst of times. Rightly we rail against those who ignore what is going on and who allow others—especially the young—to feel that this too will pass. Indignation we direct most especially at those who seek to normalize the behavior of corrupt and ruthless political elites and their enablers in the right-wing news media. "Complacent" we say of those who do their best to remain optimistic even as the culture and the entire political order are torn apart. The disinclination to undertake, even to contemplate, fundamental changes has always seemed to liberals of an activist bent to be a failure not only of imagination but of character.

Of course the most ardent and intolerant culture warriors will tell you that they and they alone are moved to think about and to effect fundamental change. Their opponents, they say, are not only complacent but are enemies of the brave new order we are summoned to build. Speak to them about climate change and the evaporation of groundwater, about the wages of so-called technological progress and the replacement of workers by machines, and they will indicate concern of the kind we have come to expect from persons who are at least somewhat alert to the fate of the planet. Ask them about inequality and the defense of indigenous communities in a rapidly globalizing world and they will express interest. But their zeal is principally reserved for issues closer to home, issues they can prosecute with some secure sense that in doing so they will be striking a blow against persons whose steadfast refusal to be intimidated or moved to instant assent they find infuriating. Culture warriors, in the academy especially, are in thrall to an ideal of solidarity. Anything less than complete submission and approval they regard as betrayal. Their instinct is to divide people into friends and enemies, with enemies figured as dispensable and hateful. Supposing themselves to be political, they have no patience for coalition building or for the difficult work of persuasion. What is to be done, they believe, is to drive away opponents and to avoid, so far as possible, self-examination. When they get together on home ground to discuss urgent matters of practical or theoretic import, the driving instinct is to learn how to speak with a single voice and to celebrate the virtues of unanimity.

The words "what is to be done?" have been sounded frequently over the last two centuries, most famously, perhaps, by the Russian writer Chernyshevsky, whose novel of that title was answered and attacked by Dostoyevsky and other nineteenth-century Russian intellectuals. Always, over the course of the debates stirred by that question, participants have differed about what was and was not possible. Some contemporary writers—including prominent writers on the left—warn against "fundamental" thinking and urge instead attention to "practical matters." Others are disdainful of "neither-liberal-nor-conservative radicalism" and efforts to stick with real-world questions that take into account what David Brooks calls the "low motivations of people as they actually are." It turns out that even persons who agree about major issues like climate change, inequality, and globalization are apt to differ about what is to be done. No less do people of goodwill who agree that intolerance is unfortunate share views about what we must do to deal with it.

In short, what is to be done will have to be decided by each of us, presumably in conversation—antagonistic or companionable—with other persons whose willingness to exchange views and proposals we can rely on. This is not the place for me to name the causes to which I contribute money or the organizations for which I volunteer my time. Suffice it to say the obvious: that I have my own view of what should be done and what I can beneficially support. I suppose I might add that for me, what is to be done is to be done with a moral intensity befitting our individual sense of what is genuinely at stake. But in bringing this book to a close I want to propose that there are also many things *not* to be done. In several respects this book has been driven by my sense that in the academy today a great many things that are *not* to be done are in fact *done*.

Not to be done:

The promulgation of ideas entertained without seriousness, that is, without any corresponding consideration of what would be entailed were they actually to be effected.

The use of ideas such as privilege, appropriation, ableism, and microaggression to sow hostility, persecute other members of a community, and make meaningful conversation impossible.

The use of the classroom and the seminar to indoctrinate students
and thus to send them off parroting views that they have not
adequately thought through or mastered.

The creation of an "us versus them" orientation, underwritten by
enemies lists and fueled by a sense that on matters for which
a consensus has been reached no dispute may be tolerated.

The weaponization of "virtue" for what Marilynne Robinson calls
"class advantage," with zealots adept mainly at trumpeting their
own superior status and making "a fetish . . . of indignation."

Finale: What is to be done—all apart from the necessary forms of
study, truth-telling, and civic engagement to which the best among
us are committed? Answer: Fight with all one's heart against what
is NOT TO BE DONE.

AN AFTERWORD

There is always unfinished business. The final word can seem final only until you recall what you left out, or change your mind. The determination to pay attention to what apparently "matters" is inevitably a form of inattention, a strategy for ignoring what you'd rather not think about. In writing *The Tyranny of Virtue* I was moved to describe my own struggles with recent developments in the culture and to wonder at the peculiar species of blindness, zealotry, and intolerance that had come to dominate much of the academic world I knew. I was aware that there were other issues to obsess about, and yet I wanted to get to the bottom of things I couldn't shake and still don't fully understand. I wanted to ask why certain good ideas—ideas generated by decent, thoughtful people—so readily fall into the hands of people who distort and betray them, why due process and a respect for evidence no longer seem especially compelling even to educated persons who are rightly outraged when the laws are broken or abused by judges and politicians they dislike, why so many are comfortable setting up a surveillance culture in which they and their friends will often be afraid to say or publish what they think.

Of course everyone in my liberal cohort is alert to the fact that the Obama presidency did not usher in a postracial era, and that the political right is waging war on our democracy. We are aware that our own liberalism has failed to achieve much that it promised: we have not integrated the schools, provided an adequate safety net for the poor, reformed police departments, or satisfactorily addressed environmental issues. Some of us also acknowledge that it is a lie to pretend that nothing at all has been done to improve conditions in the society, and so we can only wonder at the many influential writers who continue to deny what seems clear.

In a recent memoiristic essay Teju Cole writes that "part of understanding is to embrace the 'not understanding,' to inhabit a feeling of [the] uncompletable." He celebrates what he calls the imperative of the essay, with roots in the French word *essayer*: "to try or to attempt." The work he admires, and urges us to admire, remains "unresolved, unfinished; it must continue to attempt." It does not aspire or presume to be the final word. It does not presume to extinguish or triumph over the opposition.

There is a beautiful humility in Cole's writing, not something you can imitate or fully account for. I like especially his wish to be in the company of people who have a reverence for the unresolved. That sensibility seems to me foreign to the accent I hear in the standard rhetoric of the culture wars, and foreign to the posture that many of my colleagues in the American academy wish to model for their students. Instead I see, all too often, the posture of angry impatience, the presumption that everything we need to know is known, that nothing and no one can know more than we do, that those who are truly virtuous are authorized, obligated, to chastise and punish those who do not measure up. The posture of the cleansing, cancelling, and exterminating angel least becomes persons who are in the business of educating the young, who need encouragement to believe that with art and ideas it is essential to be willing to proceed, much of the time, in the dark. To dwell in doubt, to entertain and live with ambivalence. To be unsure about our own virtue. To find compelling difficult ideas that do not accord perfectly with our own.

And so I hoped, in this book, to suggest that there is something not quite right in the way we have conducted ourselves as participants in the ongoing culture wars. That many of us have lost our way, lost touch with the admirable motives that originally animated us. No need to repeat here what is plainly laid out in the book, in anecdote and analysis. But useful perhaps to note that there is work to do, and that everyone knows it. I wanted, when first I was asked to write an afterword for the paperback edition of *The Tyranny of Virtue*, to say that in the last two years things have worsened, both in the academy and in the culture at large. That though Trump and former attorney general William Barr no longer govern the country, and it is possible to imagine that respect for the rule of law and for due process will somehow survive, there are signs that suggest otherwise. Signs, too, that the intolerance and the denial of elementary facts that I anatomize in this book are by no means diminishing. That the rage for the creation of a total culture is as strong among many in the intellectual and artistic community as it had seemed to me when I was writing the book a few years ago.

In truth my first impulse, in thinking about this little afterword, was to talk about the faculty members at Princeton University who recently signed a letter demanding the setting up of what amounts to a star chamber to vet, approve, oversee, and—the implication is clear—suppress the research and writing of their colleagues if it is found to be potentially offensive or disturbing and to contradict the officially sanctioned party line at the university.

Until I decided no, I'll not go that way. No, I'll not devote so much as a paragraph to the president of Smith College, who recently put a janitor on leave after a totally baseless bias complaint was lodged against him, nor—according to the *New York Times*—offered "any public apology or amends to workers whose lives were gravely disrupted by the student's accusation." Not again try to explain why pandering of this kind is almost as ugly as the pandering that keeps alive the grievance conservatives who have made a mockery of political discourse in the last decade.

And no, I'll *not* speak about the cancellation (or "postponement") of an exhibition of paintings by Philip Guston on the grounds that particular images, of cartoonish, cigar-smoking Ku Klux Klansmen in white hoods driving around American cities in convertibles, would make viewers and museum employees feel "unsafe" and stir protests—the decision to cancel made by museum officials who themselves acknowledge that there is nothing remotely racist or offensive in the paintings.

And *no*, I'll not go into the fact that people who work in the news departments at places like the *New York Times* have used their public Twitter accounts and messaging channels to claim that an op-ed piece of which they disapprove put them in "danger" and thus that the *Times* official who published the piece should be forced to resign.

Better, I think, to note that soon after the publication of this book in the fall of 2019, several of my colleagues at Skidmore College approached me to say that they were grateful for my book, and asked me *please* not to tell anyone else about these innocent exchanges. And of course I wondered then at the courage—apparently it took some courage—of the dozens of professors and administrators at other colleges and universities who wrote me to say that things at their own schools were much worse than anything I had revealed. No wonder that, some time before his untimely death, the Polish writer Adam Zagajewski, seated one night at my dinner table with several of my friends, lamented what he called the purity tests that made him feel that the American university had come into the hands of commissars. Beware, Adam told us, of "bitter partisans with small, stiff hearts." He was thinking then of the kinds of people who screw up their faces in disdain when someone like the classicist Mary Beard mildly observes that "you want to know what people you don't agree with are saying, and . . . you don't get a sense of where the argument lies by not looking or not interacting. . . . I don't want a world in which we all agree. . . . You can't just lock the other side up and put gags around their mouths—there's too many of them!"

My friend Irving Howe, the founder and editor of *Dissent* magazine, used to say that politics too often distracts us from our "most decent instincts," and that political values are not the only values. In his great book *Politics and the Novel* Irving wondered at his admiration for the French novelist Stendhal, whom he described as "a dubious character," who gave his heart to figures distinguished by "generosity, impetuousness, gaiety." Stendhal had no feeling for those who were earnest in the prosecution of rule breakers and nonconformists, and he was exemplary in his commitment to virtues like passion and independence. Irving knew that the writers and thinkers whose works we love are always, in one degree or another, dubious characters, who write not to curry favor but to trouble us and grapple with what they don't fully understand.

I thought of this again the other day when I was reading "Some Thoughts on the Common Toad," a short 1946 essay by George Orwell that one of my sons thought might do me some good. And of course at once I felt, while reading the essay, what Orwell often inspires in me, which is the sense that he disliked authority, and the established order, and that this dislike allowed him to think for himself—allowed him, in fact, to conduct an ongoing quarrel with people in his own cohort, in the left-wing intelligentsia, whose views on many critical issues he shared. In the essay on the common toad he gives himself permission to celebrate not only toads but the miracle that is the coming of spring, a miracle especially compelling in 1946, after years of war, when Orwell found himself thinking that "this time winter is going to be permanent." And so he can't help wondering—as a progressive intellectual—whether it is somehow "wicked to take a pleasure in spring," whether it is "politically reprehensible, while we are all groaning, or at any rate ought to be groaning, under the shackles of the capitalist system, to point out that life is frequently more worth living because of a blackbird's song" or other natural phenomena which do not have "what the editors of left-wing newspapers call a class angle?"

Ridiculous, no? The thought that it might be wicked to indulge simple pleasures that have nothing to do with what many of your peers take to be the only things that are worthy of your attention. And in fact, Orwell tells us, his readers routinely send him chastising letters directed against the "political quietism" implicit in the tendency to pass up any opportunity to sow discontent or rancor. Something "reactionary" apparently in Orwell's disposition. So many of his readers contended, so that he thinks of those "who would stop me enjoying" toads and flowers, who would have him never forget even for a moment the "bombs piling up in the factories, the police. . . . prowling through the cities, the lies . . . streaming from the loudspeakers."

Of course we all know how to answer the kinds of people who would stop us enjoying what we enjoy. Know how to answer those who insist that nothing has changed for the better in the country's race relations, or in any other area of our cultural life. We know how to acknowledge, as Orwell would surely have noted if he were around, that lies and corruption are cardinal features of our political culture and that the admirable personal qualities of Barack Obama have not dramatically altered the political landscape. But we also know how to say that there is nothing to gain by denying us our weakness for this or for that, however humble, and that efforts to cancel art shows and ban or burn books will do nothing at all to meaningfully combat the actual roots of black suffering or inequality. We can even go on to say that the failure of our own liberalism—and our determination to do better—is more important by far than the notion of eliminating from our speech and artworks anything that might conceivably offend someone.

And yet we will want also to remind ourselves that Orwell was exemplary principally because he was by temperament and intelligence undeceived. Because he came out with things that stopped us in our tracks. Because—as Lionel Trilling wrote of him—"he made no effort to show that his heart was in the right place, or the left place. He was not interested in where his heart might be thought to be since he knew where it was. He was interested only in telling the truth." Did that make him a "dubious character"? Let us suppose so. There are other kinds of dubious characters, some of them admirable, in their way. And we want them around, want them in our lives, and want them as instigations to thought and feeling in the books we read and the close encounters we crave.

ACKNOWLEDGMENTS

This book began as a keynote lecture I delivered during a September 2015 conference at The New School for Social Research, where Liberal Studies director Jim Miller assembled a lively cast of respondents and, in effect, convinced me that this was a project I could not abandon. So thanks, first, to Jim, who has been a close friend and a towering intellectual presence in my life for more than forty years.

Thanks also to my dear friend Orlando Patterson, who for three decades has shaped my thinking on several of the issues covered in this book and who has demonstrated, in his own work, an exemplary commitment to scholarship, truth-telling, and intellectual courage.

My youngest son, Gabriel Boyers, has offered advice, encouragement, and criticism, scrupulously marking up the manuscript of this book and warning me of pitfalls and missteps. For his loving attention I have no adequate words of thanks.

Though I've done battle on several fronts in the course of the fifty years I've taught at Skidmore College, I owe an enormous debt of gratitude to many of those at the college who have made it possible for me to do my work as writer, teacher, writing program director, and editor of the quarterly magazine *Salmagundi*. Though I cannot name all those I'd like to thank, including current faculty members and students who continue to stir and console me, I must mention especially several former colleagues, friends of my youth

ACKNOWLEDGMENTS

who remain, in ever so many ways, indispensable: Tom Lewis, Susan Kress, Steven Millhauser, Steve Stern, and Terence Diggory. Finally, I must thank my superb editor, Colin Harrison, and my gifted, assiduous agent, Elias Altman, both of whom lighted the way to publication of this book.

ABOUT THE AUTHOR

Robert Boyers is the author of ten previous books and writes often for such magazines as *Harper's*, the *Nation*, the *New Republic*, the *American Scholar*, and the *Chronicle of Higher Education*. For fifty years he has been professor of English at Skidmore College, where he was the first Tisch Professor of Arts and Letters. He founded, and continues to edit, the quarterly magazine *Salmagundi*, and is the director of the New York State Summer Writers Institute.